0 1341 1151394 8

W9-AHQ-033

Uneasy Partners

Uneasy Partners

Multiculturalism and Rights in Canada

Janice Gross Stein

David Robertson Cameron

John Ibbitson

Will Kymlicka

John Meisel

Haroon Siddiqui

Michael Valpy

With an introduction by
the Honourable Frank Iacobucci

Wilfrid Laurier University Press

We acknowledge the support of the Canada Council for the Arts for our publishing program. We acknowledge the financial support of the Government of Canada through the Book Publishing Industry Development Program for our publishing activities.

 Canada Council   Conseil des Arts
for the Arts   du Canada

ONTARIO ARTS COUNCIL
CONSEIL DES ARTS DE L'ONTARIO

Library and Archives Canada Cataloguing in Publication

Uneasy partners : multiculturalism and rights in Canada / Janice Gross Stein ... [et al.].

Includes bibliographical references.
ISBN 978-1-55458-012-5 (pbk.)

1. Multiculturalism—Canada.   2. Civil rights—Canada.   3. Canada. Canadian Charter of Rights and Freedoms.   I. Stein, Janice

FC105.M8U54 2007   305.800971   C2007-902358-4

Contents

Acknowledgements

Bronwyn Drainie, the indefatigable editor of the *Literary Review of Canada,* called last spring to ask me to review a book. I declined politely, but I told her that I wanted to write about the controversy over the Danish cartoons, as an exemplar of the growing tension between religion and rights. Bronwyn declined politely in turn, telling me this was a well-explored subject and she doubted that I had anything new to say. I had no ready response to that comment.

Two months later, Bronwyn was back. She had reconsidered and encouraged me to try my hand at a broader essay about religion, multiculturalism and rights, particularly in a Canadian context. When I produced a draft, she turned her editor's eye to what I had written. The essay that she published in the September 2006 issue of the *LRC* resembled my original draft just enough for me to be able to claim authorship.

John Ibbitson and Haroon Siddiqui, both readers of the *LRC*, were sufficiently provoked that each wrote a column—John for *The Globe and Mail*, Haroon for *The Toronto Star*—making clear their disagreements with parts of my argument. Shortly thereafter, Brian Henderson, the director of Wilfrid Laurier University Press, called to talk about a book that would follow from the article in the *LRC*. We concurred very quickly that we wanted a multiplicity of voices. John and Haroon agreed instantly to turn their columns into articles. David

Cameron, with his customary grace, agreed to put on paper his reservations about what I had said, as did Will Kymlicka, Canada's foremost scholar of multiculturalism. Michael Valpy, after one lunch at Massey College, consented to write on religion and rights, one of his long-standing interests. John Meisel generously agreed to excerpt a chapter from his forthcoming autobiography, in which he writes about his experience as an immigrant to Canada. No eye is gentler or keener.

We all owe a special debt of gratitude to Justice Frank Iacobucci for writing the foreword to this volume. My conversations with him began one morning over breakfast at a conference and have continued over time. These conversations have been a very special treat. I am deeply grateful for his judicious thinking, his wisdom and, above all, his friendship.

Without Bronwyn Drainie and Brian Henderson, this volume would not be. Bronwyn, with the help of copy editor Madeline Koch, edited the chapters and improved them immeasurably. Brian nurtured and supported the project from the very beginning. We thank them all and hope very much that this volume contributes to the ongoing conversation about our shared future.

Janice Gross Stein
University of Toronto
April 28, 2007

Introduction

Frank Iacobucci

While growing up in Vancouver in the late 1940s, I remember vividly taking my homemade panini sandwiches out of my lunch bag and being embarrassed. My sandwiches were brimming with a combination of egg, tomatoes, cheese, peppers and prosciutto, whereas most of my Anglo-Saxon classmates had neat and tidy store-bought white bread with slim fillings. It was an awkward feeling: my sandwich being out of step with the "majority sandwich" gave me a sense of not belonging.

Later, while an undergraduate at the University of British Columbia in the 1950s, I had a disturbing conversation with my economics statistics professor, Tadek Matuszewski, for whom I was working as a teaching assistant. He asked me one day what I wanted to do with my life, and I answered that I wanted to go to law school. To my surprise, Matuszewski said I should not do that; and when I asked him why, he replied that I did not have the right name to be a lawyer. Granted, my name was, like his, difficult to spell and pronounce, but I did not understand why that should disqualify me from pursuing legal studies. Upon seeing my consternation, Matuszewski suggested that we make an appointment to see John Deutsch, then chair of the combined political science and economics department at UBC (later to become vice-chancellor of Queen's University).

We subsequently did meet with Deutsch, who was a Solomon-like figure, and I have never forgotten his answer to the question whether I should go to law school. He said, "Tadek, I think Canada is changing, and if this young man wants to go to law school, he should do so." Although satisfied with the answer, I found his response rather disquieting. If Canada was changing, what did that mean? Was the Canada I had grown up in a place in which you could not pursue a career if you had a certain type of name, gender, skin colour or religious faith?

I have since learned that, in fact, Canada was not always welcoming to women and minorities in many careers and other areas of life. It is a subject on which I have commented on many occasions with respect to the legal profession. But Deutsch was right: Canada changed, and rather dramatically, by adopting a pluralist, multicultural, equality-based approach to its social interaction. Canada's fact of diversity in its social makeup led to a policy of multiculturalism in the early 1970s (which, in my view was enlightened in concept, but somewhat wanting in practice), then to a federal statute on multiculturalism and, ultimately, to constitutional expression on multiculturalism strongly reinforced by an emphasis on equality rights for all Canadians.

That development is what this book of essays is all about. The essays are not principally historical, theoretical, philosophical or jurisprudential contributions, although those themes are reflected in the authors' treatment of their topics. In the main, the essays are practically based commentaries that view multiculturalism from different perspectives and with different themes. Both consensus and dissent on various points add to the insights and lessons that can be taken from the different writers' contributions.

The authors of these essays are distinguished journalists and academics, but they are also outstanding Canadians who have been active in various spheres of life. Their backgrounds, experience and writings on the subject of multiculturalism and related topics make them eminently qualified to offer their views. Therefore it is clearly worthwhile for all of us interested in the topic to read carefully what they have to say, even if we may disagree in whole or in part with their opinions.

That we have laws with remedies for redress on the subject of multiculturalism and equal treatment is of great importance. But as necessary as laws and remedies are, they are not sufficient. Today, there are many examples of minority culture—such as the hijab—that parallel the panini of my personal childhood experience and may create a sense of not belonging to mainstream Canadian society. Moreover, like other nations, we are faced almost daily with situations that create tension between fundamental rights such as equality and multicultural or religious freedoms. Many countries of the world are regrettably experiencing not just debates on the subject, but conflict that has led to personal injury and tragedy. Terrorism and our response to it as a democracy highlight the challenges we face in ensuring that we do not regress in our efforts to respect the individual's dignity and integrity that underlie the policies and laws regarding multiculturalism and equality. A caution is sounded in several of the essays in this book that in seeking solutions to old problems we should not overreact and invent new ones.

In spite of such concerns, the writers acknowledge the positive consequences that have followed from Canada's pluralistic or multicultural approach. They prefer the recognition of diversity and differences in culture that are embodied in multiculturalism compared to assimilationist policies that exist in other countries. Notwithstanding Canada's progress in this respect, however, historic examples are not so distant in our national memory for us to be complacent: the Chinese head tax, the internment of the Japanese and other groups during World War II, the denial of entry for Jewish refugees, episodes of racism and discrimination on grounds of gender, skin colour and religion. Worthy of special mention and a cause of national regret is the treatment of our aboriginal Canadians. The ongoing need to seek a way to eliminate the injustices and unfair treatment toward that community must be met, along with the need to find a means to coexist in a way that is mutually honourable and respectful for all citizens of Canada, aboriginal and non-aboriginal alike.

Although there is much agreement among the contributors, including consensus on what is meant by multiculturalism, one will find disagreements both in the analysis of issues and in proposed solutions to perceived problems. For example, there is disagreement on the role that religious freedom plays in multiculturalism and in relation to equality rights. There is also difference of opinion on the issue of immigration and its collision with social policies (or lack of same) that inhibit immigrant groups from participating more actively and beneficially in society. However, there is agreement that multicultural policies and developments cannot remain static and must adapt in a constructive, evolutionary manner to new pressures and conflicts, just as they have evolved since my childhood and university days in Vancouver.

My career has been in the law, thanks in part to John Deutsch's encouragement and Canada's adaptive capacity to meet the legitimate aspirations of the diverse peoples living in and coming to Canada. The law and legal institutions will be an important focus as we try to respond to the modern issues and challenges that the contributors to this volume discuss. However, lawyers and judges are not by any means the only actors in this societal play, although they have a major role to perform in deciding disputes that go to the courts or legislatures. Laws, lawyers and judges by themselves cannot effectively resolve all disputes because what is and will be at issue in present and future contests involves the seeking of a balance between fundamental individual rights, freedoms, beliefs and values, and collective societal interests. Since history has demonstrated that those rights and freedoms cannot be absolute in nature, and that collective societal interests cannot ignore individual rights, we must perforce seek an equilibrium that permits us to live together peacefully and harmoniously as members of a progressive democracy.

This equilibrium cannot be authored only by judges or, for that matter, politicians, academics, journalists, religious leaders or any other groups; ultimately it is widespread commitment by the public to seek that equilibrium that is necessary to ensure its achievement. If we Canadians can achieve that balance and the enlightenment it offers (and we have come a long way in my lifetime toward that goal), we truly will be a model for all countries of the world that aspire to a democracy in which an individual's full participation is not just free of inhibition or obstacle, but also embraced and encouraged by a profound respect for the essential human dignity of each person, regardless of his or her cultural or ethnic identity or personal characteristics.

That is a noble mission, and in that respect I congratulate and commend the authors of these essays for not only contributing to our understanding of multiculturalism and its virtues and challenges, but also for holding out the promise of making our country a better place for all of us.

The Honourable Frank Iacobucci, Q.C.
Toronto, Ontario
March 2007

Searching for Equality

Janice Gross Stein

Canadians today are proudly multicultural. Along with publicly funded health care, multiculturalism has become part of the sticky stuff of Canadian identity. It is relatively new, the latest stage in our evolution from a binational, bilingual society. An official policy of multiculturalism was first enacted in 1971, followed by the Multiculturalism Act in 1985. Section 27 of the constitution, the Canadian Charter of Rights and Freedoms, adopted in 1982, provides that the Charter "shall be interpreted in a manner consistent with the preservation and enhancement of the multicultural heritage of Canadians." In a uniquely Canadian compromise, individual and collective rights were both affirmed. The relationship between those individual and collective rights continues to be a work in progress as Canada adapts to the Charter.

These new, explicitly liberal conceptions of rights changed Canadians' view of themselves, their history, their country, their nation and their identity with consequences that are still unfolding. A "culture of rights" has gradually emerged in this country that attempts to balance individual and collective rights. In its first phase, this culture focused largely on group rights: Canadians of all backgrounds and cultures were free to be themselves. This is what we call multiculturalism. Now, I would argue, we are in a second stage, where a deeply embedded culture of individual rights is challenging cultural and religious practices that infringe on our concept of equality. Our perpetual dialogue on these issues has shifted direction.

Canada is unique among western liberal democracies in its constitutional commitment to multiculturalism. It has also done extraordinarily well in practice. Its large cities reflect an impressive range of diversity among the many cultures that live peacefully with one another. Watching World Cup soccer in Toronto provides a window into the cultural range and diversity of our largest city. As their favourite team is eliminated, people borrow cultures and switch their allegiance to the teams of other cultural communities. Bystanders are invited to join Ghanaians, French, Italians, Portuguese and Koreans who take to city streets to wave national flags in celebration. At its best, multiculturalism in Canada is inclusive, rather than exclusionary. It is open rather than closed.

Canadians generally respect difference, dislike any kind of stereotyping and make a conscious—and healthy—effort to avoid giving gratuitous offence. We are generally far more polite than our neighbours to the south and far more inclusive than many European states—Germany, France, Italy—that have old and deeply rooted cultures. Perhaps we are more inclusive because, from the outset, our national identity was never monotonic; it was given definition by the constant tension between francophone and anglophone cultures and, very belatedly, the cultures of first nations. We pride ourselves on having done things differently from the United States, with its melting-pot metaphor, its "open society" that demands assimilation and its fiercely assertive nationalism. We think that we have done better than old Europe, which treasures its past and lives uneasily with significant numbers of immigrants who are largely strangers. Generally, we do not have the squalid suburbs peopled by new immigrants that ring Paris, or the large-scale ghettoes that are visible in so many European cities. Different communities live side by side, if not exactly together, in Canada's cities, with relatively little cross-cultural violence. Canadians continue overwhelmingly to support immigration. The record is impressive and encouraging.

Despite extraordinary successes, the Canadian commitment to multiculturalism is being tested in new ways. Recent immigrants to Canada are not doing as well as previous generations. Their incomes are significantly below those of Canadians with comparable skills and they are finding it much harder to find good jobs commensurate with their education and training. Recent studies of the challenges that the Afghan, Colombian, Eritrean, Ethiopian and Jamaican communities face in Canada are troubling. Newcomers strongly identify with their homelands—rather than Canada—and insist that they face consistent patterns of social and economic exclusion. Of 176 Ethiopian young people living in Toronto, for example, two thirds identified themselves as Ethiopians first. Only 27 percent identified themselves as Canadians first, even though most were born in Canada or immigrated when they were very young. The Eritrean Canadians who were interviewed complained that they did not understand Canadian social values and felt a gap between their "two worlds" (Jiminez 2006). These kinds of results, although based on very small studies, are nevertheless a worry, since they confirm larger studies of patterns of lack of employment and income among recent new immigrants. The failure to create opportunity for new immigrants is especially worrying as Canada's population begins to age and immigrants become more important to economic growth and productivity.

Our commitment to multiculturalism is also being tested by worries about "homegrown" terrorism, the fear that acts of violence may be committed by Canadians against their own government. It hardly needs saying that the "war on terrorism" led to the informal profiling of Muslims, particularly those from South Asia and the Middle East, by security and intelligence agencies around the world. Canada was no exception. In the wake of September 11, 2001, Canada, like many other countries, passed new legislation to combat the threat of terror. Several high-profile cases have captured public attention, at times in diametrically opposite ways. Acting on information they received from Canadian police, American officials deported Maher Arar to Syria, where he was tortured. The Canadian public was appalled. As the injustice against Arar was being exposed and debated, a group of young Muslims living in Toronto was arrested and charged with conspiring to commit acts of terrorism. Now, the public was quietly concerned.

Canada, more so than other countries, is beginning to recover its usual quiet confidence and intuitive sense of balance. The courts have disallowed some of the provisions of the anti-terrorism legislation, declaring them unconstitutional. The public reacted to the arrests of some of its own citizens with restraint, tinged with a healthy dose of skepticism about the scope of the charges and the supporting evidence. There is no discernible drop in public support for immigration, nor are there demands to restrict immigrants from specific countries. It seems unlikely that legitimate concern about the threat of terrorism will spill over into a generalized and broad-scale attack against multiculturalism. Canada is most assuredly not Europe.

The principal challenge to multiculturalism, in my view, lies elsewhere. Multiculturalism is being tested by a global resurgence of religious orthodoxy. Coming after several centuries of enlightenment, science, a culture of progress and the embedding of liberalism in the West, the flourishing of religious orthodoxy is surprising. It is also an important comment on the unfulfilled promise of the enlightenment and of secular societies. Religious orthodoxy is growing in poorer societies in the South, it is growing in some rich societies such as the United States, and it travels easily with some diasporic communities that bridge societies and cultures. It is happening in Christianity, in Islam, in Judaism and in Hinduism, where lines of division between "them" and "us" are being drawn more sharply than they were half a century ago.

This global resurgence of religious orthodoxy cannot leave Canada untouched. As religious orthodoxy grows, it spills over into politics and society in unexpected ways and challenges other cultures. The most obvious fault line is the tension between the treatment of women and homosexuals in different religions and cultures, and their rights to equality that are given voice through the Charter. Multiculturalism is being tested in part because Canadians are uncertain about what limits, if any, there are to embedding diverse religious and cultural traditions within the Canadian context. We know pretty well what the "multi" in multicultural means, but are much less confident about the "culture." Does culture in Canada mean just a respect for pluralism and difference? Or is there more? Have we produced a broader set of shared values that must, at some point, bump up against the diversity and difference that we celebrate? Do Canadians share values that go beyond the much-abused—and at times offensive—concept of tolerance? How do we recognize and respect religious traditions and cultures that systemically discriminate against women? Against homosexuals? This conversation is now bubbling up in Canada as it is in other parts of the world.

Some of the conversation that is taking place around the world is, on the surface, simply silly. There is a great deal of talk right now about what women wear. Jack Straw, the foreign secretary in the United Kingdom, complained about the niqab, the full-face veil that some Muslim women choose to wear. The argument, allegedly, was that the niqab creates a sense of distance and separation between the veiled woman and her interlocutor (Cowell 2006). The debate about women's dress echoes eerily in Dubai, one of the most multicultural cities in the Middle East. Here, too, a debate has begun about the limits of multiculturalism. The local English-language newspaper, *7Days*, editorialized against the growing disrespect for Muslim customs: "Too much [female] flesh on show is wrong in a Muslim country at any time—but offense is being felt especially during Ramadan," argued a front-page editorial headlined "Show Some Respect" (Fattah 2006; see also *7Days* 2006).

These two debates seem almost mirror images of one another. In Britain, it is the majority that is uncomfortable with the habits of the minority, while in Dubai, it is the minority that is uncomfortable with the habits of the majority. (Emiratis are actually a minority in the city of Dubai, which has almost a million foreign residents who are ineligible for citizenship.) In both countries, the politics of cultural identity, a complex politics embedded in larger tropes of insecurity and fear of assimilation, quickly focused on the clothes that women wear or don't wear.

On the surface, this is a conversation that we in Canada would not and should not have. We have a healthy respect for what is public and what is private and what a person wears is her private decision, not an appropriate focus for public regulation or comment. We would not think of enforcing restrictions against Hebrew skullcaps, Christian crosses or Muslim hijabs in our public schools, as France has done. We are interested, at times fascinated, by differences in dress, food, song and dance, and we actively celebrate these differences in Canada.

Nevertheless, the seemingly silly debate about what women wear covers a deeper issue, an issue that runs just beneath the surface.

Almost all the world's great religions insist that women must be covered, that they must be modestly dressed and that they must behave with appropriate modesty. Rarely is there a debate about the modesty of men's dress or men's behaviour. The debate about modesty—on all sides—is a surrogate for a much larger, more difficult and more serious debate about the equality of women, about their rights within the envelope of cultural and religious practices. Some women from all religions tell me that they cover up because they fear their fathers or their uncles or their brothers, and therefore it is easier and safer to acquiesce. Others, again from all religious traditions, tell me that they cover up as a mark of identity, as a symbol of authenticity, as a sign of respect. It is more than a passing curiosity that, in all these religions, it is men who choose these forms of authenticity, who give content and meaning to "respect."

It is difficult in any of the foundational texts of the three great monotheistic religions to find instructions that require women to cover themselves extensively. Traditions of women's dress have evolved over time as society has evolved, and evolutionary psychologists have provided compelling explanations as to why men would want women, especially their partners, to be covered in public. The covering of women began not as religious observance, but as a sign of class difference. Upper class women were able to wear the long, flowing robes that their less fortunate female counterparts, who had to work in the fields, could not.

Yet we accept these arguments about authenticity within our broader tradition of multiculturalism and rarely engage the deeper argument about the systematic differences in the treatment of men and women. We do not talk in public about the coincidence that it is women who are covered, irrespective of the religious tradition. Nor do we talk about the belief, common to all religions, that women are responsible for inciting the lust of men. I suspect that we don't go beyond polite conversation about the cultural and religious origins of women's dress because we are socialized to recognize and respect difference. We are trained to be multicultural.

There is more than a sniff of smugness in our celebration of our successes as a multicultural society. Is respect for difference being polluted by a reluctance to set limits, to give positive content to what and who we are as well as to what we recognize and respect? These questions are not important if multiculturalism is largely restricted to the celebration of song, dance, poetry, literature, language and food. It is these kinds of celebration that are the stuff of the official policy of multiculturalism in Canada's large cities. In Toronto, on a warm July weekend afternoon, residents can choose among a Brazilian street festival, the Corso Italia Toronto Fiesta or Afrofest. Eating food that sizzles on street corners, dancing to Latin music or listening to African song is an enriching experience. This is easy multiculturalism, multi-culturalism light, which raises no hard questions at all.

But the hard questions are there, creating quiet unease as real divisions creep into the debate about cultural and religious distinctive-ness. How far can respect for difference go? When does it constrain freedom of expression? That issue boiled over when cartoons from Denmark that Muslims considered defamatory were published, but anti-Semitic cartoons have provoked similar debates. Freedom of expression is a fundamental right, one that underpins all the elements of our democratic practices. Does freedom of expression permit one group to insult and stereotype another? How far can religious and cultural stereotyping go before it becomes incitement to hatred? In Canada, we have struggled for decades to find answers to these questions and our judges have interpreted legislation to strike a delicate balance between freedom of expression and the avoidance of racially, culturally and religiously motivated hate.

Some of these issues open the door to the discussion of the role of the state, a discussion that does not happen easily in Canada. Does respect for different cultures, for example, extend to the public sanc-tioning of religious courts as voluntary courts for arbitration, courts that use religious traditions that are likely to violate the rights of women? That discussion raged in Ontario until the government re-fused to permit the creation of Islamic courts and simultaneously withdrew its sanction of orthodox Jewish legal courts operating under public authority. The government decided that it would not officially recognize religious legal practices in arbitration even though these courts will, of course, continue to be used in private on a voluntary basis. No other outcome is conceivable in a society where freedom of religion is guaranteed as a Charter right.

Yet, even here, we may be taking comfort too easily. Private use of these courts may not be wholly voluntary; some women may have very little choice given the authority structure within their cultural communities. In a study of the Eritrean community, admittedly a very small study, every female respondent said that she had no trust in her community and would not reach out to traditional community structures to resolve personal, family or social conflicts. Turning a blind eye to private use of law courts on a voluntary basis is, at one level, the only option available to a society like ours that respects the boundaries between private and public space. Even as we turn away, however, we know that women and gays are systematically disadvantaged in many of these private courts that use religious law or tradition interpreted through structures of authority within communities. We draw a line at violence and abuse, and manage these violations of rights through the criminal code, but let almost everything else fall under the rubric of multiculturalism. The Charter, of course, does not apply to private space. Our rights culture, in other words, stops at the door.

These kinds of issues take us to the terrain where the law has not spoken, where it is thus far silent. How committed are "we" in Canada to the secularization of public space? Do we welcome multiple religious symbols in public squares in December or do we ban them all? How far can religious practice and celebration extend into public space? Are we impoverishing ourselves collectively when we banish Christmas trees from public squares in an effort not to offend Jews, Hindus and Muslims? Is the answer to celebrate the religious festivals of all communities or to celebrate none?

These issues of cultural and religious iconography are at most seasonal vexations that communities treat with appropriate good humour, consideration and bemusement. They pale in comparison to the conflict between the right to freedom of religion and equality rights, both of which are embedded in our constitution through the Charter of Rights and Freedoms. But our approach to even these symbolic conflicts tells us a great deal about what meaning we give to multiculturalism and how we understand equality rights in our diverse society.

We are not the only society that is debating these issues. And we are having several debates simultaneously. The debate in Quebec, not surprisingly, is different in its focus than in English Canada. In Quebec, multiculturalism is joined at the hip to concern about the survival of the French language and Québécois culture in an English-speaking and increasingly Spanish-speaking North America. In continental Europe—in France and Germany, for example—the debate is louder, more strident, openly entangled in questions of how the "other" can become the self, how the stranger can become less strange. Germans speak openly of how important it is that "newcomers" learn German history and culture as well as the language. France makes no claims to multiculturalism, and openly insists on a culture of *"laïcité,"* or secularism, with an enforced dress code in its public schools. The debate in Britain is closer to our own. Britain celebrates its diversity, its many cultures, in theory if not in practice. Here, too, however, a new debate has erupted in London's magazines and salons about the limits to diversity that need to be put in place so that a culture of civil disagreement, rejection of violence and engaged citizenship can be created across the country's often segregated neighbourhoods. The British refer to this debate as "citizenship plus."

We in Canada pride ourselves that we have done better, that ours is a multicultural society that works. And it does work, by and large. Nevertheless, I suspect that we do draw some boundaries in Canada. We are most comfortable with those boundaries that we have enshrined over the years in the rule of law and, more recently, in the Charter of Rights and Freedoms. We not only celebrate differences, but we also value the human rights that define the quality of our democratic norms and practice. So far, so good. Where we are reluctant to go, however, is the conflict between universal human rights that we treasure and different religious and cultural traditions. One obvious fault line, one that we have tended to tiptoe around, is the rights of women in different religious and cultural traditions in our midst.

Women in Canada are guaranteed equal rights and an equal voice in the determination of our shared vision of the common good. We respect rights and we respect diversity, but at times the two compete. Canadians are less accepting of multiculturalism when it conflicts with gender equality. In a recent poll, 81 percent of those surveyed felt that immigrants should adapt to mainstream Canadian beliefs about the rights and role of women (Environics 2006). In other words, Canadians do draw a line around multiculturalism when it puts women's rights at risk. They give higher priority to equality rights than to freedom of religion.

Canadian laws are very clear in a few of the cases where rights compete. Multiculturalism stops, for example, when women are subjected to physical abuse by their partners. Harpal Johl, a counsellor working with a group of Indo-Canadian men living in Vancouver, explains that "their belief system" sees nothing wrong with the use of physical violence against a family member. Johl emphasized that domestic violence occurs in every ethnic community and cuts across all social and economic groups but conceded nevertheless that "certain cultural traits unique to South Asian society allowed domestic violence to fester and ignite" (Armstrong 2006). When he works with his clients, he counsels cultural change in the treatment of women.

On issues of domestic violence, the law speaks clearly and treats physical abuse as criminal behaviour. Other issues are far less clear. What to do about private religious schools, for example, that do not teach the official curriculum and receive no support from governments? In 2006, a school board in the Outaouais region in Quebec complained that the provincial curriculum was not being followed in an evangelical school. Supporters of Église Évangélique, affiliated with l'Association des églises évangéliques du Québec, argued that the school teaches a "world view" that was essential for their students. "We offer a curriculum based on a Christian world view," said the chair of its curriculum committee (Rogers 2006). After an inquiry, Quebec's Ministère de l'Éducation told unlicensed Christian evangelical schools that they must teach Darwin's theory of evolution and sex education or the schools would be closed. The legal requirement that children are required to go to school until the age of sixteen and that they are required to follow the official curriculum overrode—at least in the view of the Ministère de l'Éducation—the right to freedom of religion in the schools. Apparently not so in neighbouring Ontario. Here, according to Elaine Hopkins, the executive director of the Ontario Federation of Independent Schools, schools are not required to teach either evolution or sex education.

Education in Canada falls under provincial jurisdiction, so the different readings of the right to freedom of religion in education are not surprising. The different experience in these two neighbouring provinces illustrates the spectrum of responses to freedom of religion in public and private space. Ontario treats private space as entirely private, at least in elementary education. Quebec does not; it insists that its rules on curricular content apply to wholly private, independently funded schools as well as to public education.

This tension between private and public space gets played out in different ways as we think about multiculturalism, religion and rights when rights compete directly with one another. Can private schools meet government criteria by teaching the official curriculum but segregate girls in separate classrooms for religious or cultural reasons? Should schools that do so receive any government funding? Should universities, for example, make space available to student groups that segregate women in worship? The University of Toronto agreed to provide space for Jewish and Islamic services that separate men from women while McGill University refused to do so. Both are public institutions and, in both cases, the arguments are interesting. The University of Toronto considered that it was leasing its space to student groups, who exercise autonomy in the way they use the space. McGill argued that it was inappropriate for a public institution to allow its space to be used for religious purposes and encouraged students groups to find space off campus. In neither case was the issue of women's rights in public institutions openly joined. The focus was on private or public space and on contractual arrangements, not on rights.

To the surprise of many Canadians who come from quite different ends of the political spectrum, the relationship between equality rights and the right to freedom of religion is now on the public agenda. The most recent controversy focused on whether public officials can refuse to perform official duties because of private religious beliefs. When same-sex marriage was legalized in Canada in 2005, the legislation specifically exempted clergy who objected on religious grounds from the obligation to perform same-sex marriages. In the autumn of 2006, the press reported that the new Conservative government was considering a defence of religions act to allow public officials, such as justices of the peace, to refuse to perform same-sex marriages. The measures are also intended to protect the right to freedom of expression of those who criticize gay behaviour because it contravenes religious teachings or to prevent those who refuse to do business with gay-rights organizations from being brought before human rights tribunals (Ibbitson, Curry and Laghi 2006). In British Columbia, the Human Rights Tribunal has upheld the right of the Knights of Columbus to refuse to rent their hall to two women who were planning to marry.

A firestorm of controversy erupted. The federal government does not have the constitutional authority to legislate on the solemnization of marriage, an issue of clear provincial jurisdiction. Any attempt to introduce legislation to allow justices of the peace or civil service commissioners to refuse to perform same-sex marriages because of their private religious beliefs would be very unlikely to survive a challenge in the courts. The constitutional technicality should not obscure the larger conflict about how far the right to freedom of religion and the right to freedom of expression should intrude into public space, even when they compromise fundamental equality rights. This kind of legislation, similar to a private member's bill introduced in the Alberta legislature, would permit freedom of religion to trump the right to equality, even in public space. It would compromise equality rights in the most fundamental way by allowing public officials to invoke their private religious views to refuse to perform their public duties. To put the point more colloquially, it would legalize discrimination in public spaces. Even though the government has abandoned any attempt to introduce the legislation, that it was considered at all shows how far the debate has swung as proponents seek to extend the right to religious freedom ever more deeply into public space.

At the other end of the spectrum, advocates of equality rights are seeking to engage churches, synagogues and mosques about the status of those rights behind their doors. Their arguments treat these religious organizations as quasi-public institutions, institutions that enjoy special status and receive special benefits from the state, mainly in the form of tax concessions. Paradoxically, these kinds of conflicts are most intense, not in those branches of religion where literal readings of text provide little room for interpretation or deviation, but rather in those that are most responsive to Canadian society even as they cherish their traditions.

These conflicts are not abstract, but very personal to me. When I challenged my rabbi recently about his longstanding refusal to give women in my congregation the right to participate fully and equally in religious services, he argued: "I have not taken the position of 'separate but equal,' although I believe that a case can be made for this perspective. I have not argued for a fully egalitarian expression of Judaism, although I believe that a case can be made for this perspective. Instead, I have pressed for increased inclusion."

Indeed, under his leadership our congregation now permits a greater degree of involvement for women in daily services, in public readings and in leading parts of the liturgy. These are far more than cosmetic changes, but to me, as significant as these changes are, they are not enough. Women are still not counted as members of the group of ten people that must be present before prayers can begin. Only men count. I have had the extraordinary experience of sitting in a chapel and watching the leader of prayers count the men in the room, his eyes sliding over me as he counted. For all intents and purposes, not only did I not count, but I was invisible. When only nine men were present along with eight women, we waited—endlessly it seemed to me—for the tenth man.

I do not think, contrary to my rabbi, that any argument at all can be made for separate but equal treatment. Here I cannot follow his logic. These kinds of arguments have a long and inglorious history of discrimination that systematically disadvantages some part of a community. Arguments of separate but equal treatment underpinned apartheid in South Africa and the worst kind of racial discrimination in the southern United States. Nor are the theological or logical merits of an argument for "greater inclusion" obvious to me. I understand these as credible political arguments but they are hardly convincing moral arguments. I fail to understand why women should be given greater "privileges," but should not count as equals in constituting a prayer group. What principle is at work here? Where is the language of equality and rights? Even though the Charter strictly applies only to public space, I take its spirit and its values seriously.

My religious obligation clashes openly and directly with values that I hold deeply as a Canadian. Fortunately, there are Jewish congregations in the city in which I live that are fully egalitarian. My cultural and religious community is sufficiently pluralistic that I can choose among a wide variety of options. A resolution of my personal dilemma is available to me—I can vote with my feet—but the issue is public as well as private.

These religious institutions that systemically discriminate against women are recognized, at least implicitly, by governments through the special privileges that they are given. Religious institutions do not pay property tax and most receive charitable status from the federal government. If religious institutions enjoy a significant advantage because they are exempt from property tax, are these wholly private institutions? If religious institutions are able to raise funds more easily because governments give a tax benefit to those who contribute, are religious practices wholly private even when they benefit from the public purse? Are discriminatory religious practices against women and gays a matter only for religious law, as is currently the case under Canadian law, which protects freedom of religion as a Charter right? Or should the equality rights of the Charter have some application when religious institutions are officially recognized and advantaged in fundraising? Does it matter that the Catholic church, for example, which has special entitlements given to it by the state and benefits from its charitable tax status, refuses to ordain women as priests?

We have thus far been unwilling in Canada to ask these kinds of questions. Not so in Britain. The Equal Opportunities Commission is now looking at how the government can address the discriminatory treatment of women in religious institutions (Woodward 2006). In Canada, the discussion makes us uncomfortable. It is politically incorrect, not respectful of different cultures and religious traditions. Like other societies, we in Canada live with some convenient hypocrisies. I have deliberately chosen a personal issue—the issue of women's participation in religious services in my own synagogue—to open up this difficult discussion of the desirable limits to multiculturalism and religious freedom. A fellow board member in my synagogue who was deeply affronted by my criticism repeatedly asked me whether I truly meant that our synagogue discriminated against women and gays. How could this be, he insisted, when our practices were consistent with religious law? When I replied—as gently as I could—that religious law itself was in this case discriminatory, the unexpected connection was both surprising and disconcerting. My colleague's surprise is one of the costs of silence.

Some urge silence and patience until a new social consensus emerges. Opening up difficult conversations too early can fracture communities, inflict deep wounds and do irreversible damage to those who are most open to experimentation. In my own congregation, I have been counselled for the last five years to be patient. Give it time, I'm told, and the synagogue will become fully egalitarian. I find it hard to be patient into the indefinite future, with no commitments from my religious leadership. I find it hard as a Canadian to affirm religious practices weekly that I know full well are discriminatory. I find it hard as a Jew to separate myself from values that I cherish as a Canadian. I worry that distance will grow between the two cultures unless we keep a civil but difficult conversation going.

There is no question that there is a conflict between equality rights, on the one hand, and the right to freedom of religion, on the other. The law recognizes that conflict, but we need to ask hard questions about the balance between them. My synagogue is ahead of comparable synagogues in the city, even though it is behind others in North America. If I am expected to be patient, almost endlessly patient, then religious leaders must be cognizant of the responsibilities of their organizations to engage with Canadian culture and values as they are expressed in our most fundamental laws. That these values are liberal, that at the extreme they protect individual rights at the expense of collective traditions, is a clear expression of what Canada has become in the last several decades. It is the "culture" in our multicultural richness.

There is, as we know, often no perfect solution when rights compete with one another. Canadians do not tolerate deliberate incitement of hatred by one group against another. The law is careful; it sets criteria of deliberate intention to spread hate and does not punish a spontaneous utterance that was not intended and willful. It does, however, quite deliberately limit freedom of speech when that speech becomes hatred and incitement to violence. Thus far, Canadian courts have been more willing to limit freedom of speech than they have freedom of religion. That it speaks in one instance and is silent in the other is not a matter of legal principle but of social context. Social contexts change.

The silence of the law on the competition between the right to freedom of religion and equality rights leaves a large space for collective and individual responsibility. What responsibilities do leaders of religious and cultural communities have, for example, when some members preach the use of violence against others? Do religious and cultural leaders within these communities have an obligation to move to stop this kind of preaching when they hear it?

Religious leaders certainly have no legal obligation to do so. We are all individually responsible for our own actions. I think that they do have a civic obligation to do so as Canadians who share the consensus against incitement to hate and the respect for diversity. Haroon Siddiqui (2006) argued eloquently in his column in the *Toronto Star* that community leaders have no special obligation. In the wake of the arrests of seventeen Muslims in Toronto in June 2006, he warned, correctly in my opinion, against assertion of collective Muslim guilt, but argued, incorrectly in my view, that community leaders have no responsibility at all for what members do. "Any time some Muslims somewhere commit an atrocity, a chorus of voices demands of Muslims everywhere: 'What do *you* have to say about this?' They should have to say nothing more than Christians or Jews or Hindus must for the wrongs of their co-religionists.... Muslims are also told to 'take responsibility' for their deviants, 'root out their extremists,' 'weed out the radicals, etc.' How are they supposed to do that?" Siddiqui asks. "By becoming vigilantes?"

These are good questions that deserve serious deliberation. Did the local imam in the mosque in Toronto, Ali Hindy, where fiery sermons inciting violence were routinely heard, have a responsibility to challenge the preacher, to dispute the interpretation of the text, and to warn the young people of the risks and the dangers? I think that he did. That kind of behaviour is not vigilantism. It is a responsible debate about the limits of religious freedom in a Canadian culture that abjures hate. It is also a conversation about the responsibilities of those who enjoy religious freedom in a multicultural society.

I can and do ask myself about responsibility. Although the two issues—systemic discrimination against women and incitement to hatred—are different not only in degree but also in kind, I nevertheless think that I do have an obligation to challenge my rabbi. I have been asked again and again why I do not simply leave my synagogue and go to one that is fully egalitarian, which respects women's rights and those of the gay community. Liberalism can be construed as protecting the autonomy of the individual, the capacity to make meaningful choices. As long as I have alternatives, as long as our society is sufficiently pluralistic and open so that I can find a synagogue where my rights are respected, collectively, the argument goes, we have no problem. It is only when there are no choices, when religious institutions or cultural practices systematically violate rights and deprive individuals of their choices, that society acting through the state may have grounds to intervene.

This argument is problematic from two quite different perspectives. First, it is not at all clear that governments would intervene even if choice were severely restricted and religious institutions were uniformly discriminatory. They have not done so in the past, arguing through their silence that freedom of religion makes all practices short of violence and abuse permissible. In this sense, the presence of choice in a pluralistic society simply muddies the debate, although I am personally very grateful that I do have choice. Second, religious and cultural institutions change slowly. They are by nature conservative, rightfully laggards rather than leaders. Religion tends to give a franchise to the past and, in this sense, will always reflect both the cultural and counter-cultural in the society in which it lives. That it gives a franchise to the past does not remove its responsibility to engage with the present.

Religious and cultural practices that live over time are very much like legal regimes that do adapt and evolve as social conditions change, as new norms develop, and as pressure builds. They respond to pressures both from without and within. In this sense, my behaviour is neither vigilantism nor obstructionist nor disloyal, as it is occasionally labelled by some in my religious and cultural community. It is designed to provoke responsible debate about the boundaries of religious freedom in a Canadian culture that embeds equality and human rights in our most fundamental laws.

Much of this essay has dealt with religious practices that discriminate against women and gays in an age when Canadian laws enshrine equality rights as well as freedom of religion and freedom of expression. It may seem strange to devote so much attention to religious practices in the context of a larger discussion about multiculturalism and rights. Indeed, critics have alleged that the conflicts I am writing about are tensions between religion and rights, not cultures and rights. I am afraid that is too easy a response. The practical and conceptual boundaries between religion and culture are porous. In theory and in practice, they bleed into one another.

Many, although not all, new immigrants to Canada bring with them a deep commitment to religious practice, just as immigrants did a generation and a century ago. This kind of commitment is intensifying as religious orthodoxy grows and deepens globally. Today immigrants— and second- and third-generation Canadians—build bridges and stay connected to communities back home in an era when communication is fast and inexpensive. Under these conditions, it becomes extraordinarily difficult to separate culture and religion, which are deeply intermingled and expressed through shared practices.

It is also true that for some communities, religious affiliation and practice shape culture. It is not ethnic identification but religious affiliation that is the primary construct and the most powerful form of identity. In these cases religion becomes culture, often to a degree that is incomprehensible to an outsider. The concept of a "secular Jew" may seem to be an oxymoron, but it is widely accepted as a primary identification by many within the Jewish community. In the Muslim world, it is no longer strange to hear talk of "secular Muslims"; a prominent speaker at a recent conference in Vancouver identified himself precisely that way. Used this way, is Muslim or Jew a religious or a cultural identity? It is most likely both, hopelessly intermingled and cross-pollinated over the centuries. To draw neat boundaries between religion and culture is to miss this dynamic.

CONCLUSION

We are at one of those hinge moments. The widespread movement of ideas and people is global, enriching our society and providing a marvellous opportunity for Canada to grow and develop in the next few decades. A vibrant immigration is especially important as our population ages. If we are to make the most of that opportunity, however, we will have to build a deep rather than a shallow multiculturalism. Shallow multiculturalism is a veneer, official policy but not embedded practice, and can have damaging consequences for a democratic society. What I call deep multiculturalism is a resource and a strength for a democratic society in an era of globalization. Multiculturalism in Canada needs to be capable of meeting three core challenges.

First, it is important that we join the discussion of equality rights and cultural difference with explicit attention to the overlay of social and economic inequalities. Multiculturalism is shallow when social and economic inequalities reinforce and strengthen cultural difference and then fuel a sense of victimization within an impoverished minority. From this sense of grievance can grow frustration, anger and, occasionally, an explosion of violence. England and France, each in their own way, have recently undergone variants of this kind of experience. Each is now looking hard at the economic and social disparities among cultural and religious communities. We need to do the same in Canada. The difficult experiences that many new immigrants to Canada are having in our large cities—the barriers to employment, the inadequate funding of assistance to settlement—are all important issues that merit our serious attention. It is cold comfort to new immigrants that we in Canada are interested in their songs and food when they cannot find jobs. Multiculturalism, whatever else it is about, also has to be about successful entry into the Canadian economy.

Second, deep multiculturalism builds bridges across cultures, while shallow multiculturalism strengthens each culture within its own boundaries. As things stand now in Canada, each community can treasure its own language, its history, its songs, its literature and its religious practices. But one community does not necessarily learn about another, and then multiculturalism can have perverse effects. It can strengthen the fences around each community and, in so doing, help to seal one community off from another. The Cantle Report, issued in England after riots broke out in three northern industrial towns in 2001, found "separate educational arrangements, community and voluntary bodies, employment, places of worship, language, social and cultural networks" resulted in communities that "do not seem to touch at any point" (Home Office 2001). More recently, Trevor Philips, chair of the UK's Commission for Racial Equality, warned that much of Britain was "sleepwalking its way toward segregation" (Caldwell 2006, 47).

How do cultural and religious communities live together in Canada's cities? Are they segregated, living side by side rather than together? How often does one join in the other's celebrations? Where do communities share public space? There are some worrying trends in multiculturalism in Canada. Some children, for example, go only to their community schools until they are ready for post-secondary education, worship at community institutions, go to community summer camps, play soccer or hockey within their own communities, and make friends only with kids who have similar cultural connections. The pattern in Britain is being replicated in some of our communities in Canadian cities. Young people from different cultural communities tell me that they met first when they came to university. Even there, some tell me, students clubs tend to form around cultural and religious communities, and it can be difficult for students to meet and befriend students from different cultures. This kind of evidence, while only anecdotal, is troubling.

These closed patterns of associations may well not provide enough opportunity to talk *across* cultures. To the credit of my synagogue, at that same synagogue that refuses to give women equal rights, the rabbinical leadership has been extraordinarily aware of the importance of building bridges and have led inter-faith dialogue and shared services among Muslims, Christians and Jews. Institutions that occupy public space have special responsibilities to build these bridges among cultural communities, to encourage different communities to come together around shared issues. Universities, for example, need to do a much better job of structuring shared experiences and of encouraging conversations across cultural divides among their students. What we in Canada can learn from the experience of others is that cross-cultural talk does not always happen by accident.

Finally, we need to make more robust the meaning of "culture" in our experience of multiculturalism. We have to make explicit the contradictions between cultural or religious traditions and the rule of law in Canada, when such contradictions exist. There are very large areas where there are no tensions at all. But where they do exist, we cannot turn away. We have to begin the uncomfortable and difficult discussion of the conflict between values and work very hard to find an appropriate balance. Communities that systematically discriminate against women and gays, whether they are cultural—such as the Sikh community from Punjab living in Vancouver or the Eritrean community in Toronto—or religious, may find legal protection in the freedom of religion but they should not find it in multiculturalism, where the law currently is silent. That the Charter applies only to public space does not vitiate the broad support Canadians today give to equality rights, not only in public but in private life as well.

Finding the appropriate balance is no easy task. The Charter officially recognizes multiculturalism at the same time as it guarantees equality. The balance, therefore, is always negotiable, part of an endless process of recalibrating that reflects our evolving understanding of the social contract among fellow citizens. To expect to strike that balance easily or without controversy is naive, but to seek refuge in silence when the conversation becomes too difficult is irresponsible. In Canada, of late, we have turned away from difficult conversation too easily. Some of my fellow contributors to this volume will write about the virtues of silence and the risks of conversation. On this we disagree. It is difficult to defend silence to women, newly arrived in Canada, locked into traditional authority structures within their community and afraid to seek help.

There will be times when despite our best efforts at civil conversation, we will fail to find an appropriate balance among competing rights, and conflict will explode. When we cannot find that balance— I have failed miserably thus far with my own rabbi—we need to make clear that the conflict is real and serious. We are not simply Jews or Hindus or Muslims or Christians or Indians or Pakistanis or Somalis or Eritreans or Germans, we are Jews and Hindus and Muslims and Christians and Indians and Pakistanis and Somalis and Eritreans and Germans who live—together—in Canada. That we live in Canada matters. How we live together in Canada matters. Our sense of what Canada is, our commitment to the Charter and to human rights, what Canada gives us and what we owe it, is what we collectively bring to each new cultural encounter. It is what gives meaning to Canadian culture within the tradition of multiculturalism.

REFERENCES

Armstrong, Jane. 2006. "Counselling Cultural Change." *Globe and Mail*, November 4, p. A16.

Caldwell, Christopher. 2006. "After Londonistan." *New York Times Magazine*, June 25, p. 47.

Cowell, Alan. 2006. "British Leader Splits Nation with His Call to Raise Veils." *New York Times*, October 7, p. A6.

Environics. 2006. "Canadians' Views of the Muslim Community Are Positive: Trudeau Foundation Poll." Environics Research Group Poll for the Trudeau Foundation, November. http://erg.environics.net/media _room/default.asp?aID=618 (March 2007).

Fattah, Hassan M. 2006. "Beyond Skimpy Skirts, A Rare Debate on Identity." *New York Times*, October 19, p. A4.

Home Office (United Kingdom). 2001. "Community Cohesion: A Report of the Independent Review Team," chaired by Ted Cantle. http://www .communities.gov.uk/index.asp?id=1502708 (March 2007).

Ibbitson, John, Bill Curry and Brian Laghi. 2006. "Tories Plan to Protect Same-Sex Opponents." *Globe and Mail*, October 4, p. A1.

Jiminez, Marina. 2006. "Canada's Welcome Mat Worn, Immigrant Studies Find." *Globe and Mail*, October 20, p. A12.

Rogers, David. 2006. "Evangelical Schools Ordered to Teach Darwin." *National Post*, October 24, pp. A1, A8.

7Days. 2006. "Show Some Respect." http://www.7days.ae/2006/10/03/show-some-respect.html (March 2007).

Siddiqui, Haroon. 2006. "Muslim-Bashing Dilutes Our Democratic Values." *Toronto Star*, June 11, p. A17.

Woodward, Will. 2006. "Integrate, Blair Tells Radical Muslims." *Globe and Mail*, December 9, p. A2.

Don't Blame Multiculturalism

Haroon Siddiqui

"Canada is a nation of immigrants that hates immigrants." So wrote Irving Abella, eminent historian and former president of the Canadian Jewish Congress.

"Canadians want immigration but not immigrants." So said Ratna Omidvar, executive director of The Maytree Foundation, one of Canada's leading think tanks on immigrant integration.

Both Abella and Omidvar are being mischievous, of course. But it is part of the sociology of Canada, indeed most immigrant nations, that the last person in wants the door shut right behind him or her. It has long been part of our popular mythology that new immigrants commit too many crimes or rip off the social welfare system, or that they are just the wrong sort to have been allowed into the country, being either "unassimilable" or unwilling to do what they must to integrate, a failure made worse in recent years by an official policy of multiculturalism that puts little or no onus on minorities to become fully Canadian.

The complainers are not just the Canadian born but also older and well-settled immigrants, who also come to believe that the newer immigrants are decidedly not of the same calibre as they themselves were, and that too many are making too many demands of others and doing too little adjusting themselves.

Yet it is the genius of Canada and Canadians that such bar-room wisdom is rarely, if ever, elevated to public policy. Canadians remain committed not only to high levels of immigration but also to a non-discriminatory selection process. Unlike in Europe, no anti-immigrant or racist political party in Canada can hope to win an election. The Reform Party tried that in the early 1990s—advocating immigration only from "traditional sources," meaning Europe—but soon developed the electoral sense to ditch the proposal. One of my most memorable journalistic moments was to witness the denouement of Reform leader Preston Manning's political transformation in 2000 when he addressed a Chinese Canadian rally at SkyDome in Toronto and wished the multitude a happy Chinese new year—in broken Cantonese. One cannot imagine the leader of a right-of-centre political party in France and Germany wishing Happy Eid to French and German Muslims, let alone doing so in Arabic and Turkish.

It is part of the magic of Canada and Canadians that poll after poll shows overwhelming public support for pluralism and multiculturalism. The public's only qualifier is that immigrants had better respect Canadian values, including gender equity. But even such caveats are born of the false assumption, often embedded in the poll question and hence in the responses, that immigrants do not subscribe to the same values as we do. Of course, they do. Those who do not would, at some point, run afoul of the law and face the consequences.

Unease with immigration and multiculturalism—one serving as a lightning rod for the other—inevitably rises during economic slowdowns, as happened during the early 1990s, or in times of troubles, such as the post–September 11 period. It is, therefore, not surprising that we have been having spirited debates lately on various aspects of immigration and multiculturalism, especially relating to the Canadian Muslim community (pegged at 580,000 in the 2001 census but estimated at 750,000 as of 2006). The current public discourse, however, is not limited to issues pertaining to that minority alone but covers a wide range of topics that concern the common good. The more the debate the merrier, obviously. It is in that spirit that I approach the topics under discussion in this book.

GENDER EQUITY

Houses of Worship

I agree with Janice Gross Stein that the state is not neutral in the uneasy balance between two competing constitutional rights—that of gender equality and the right to freedom of religion. Ottawa grants charitable tax status to religious institutions that discriminate against women in a variety of ways—allowing them only in the pews but not the pulpit, refusing them the right to perform marriages, ignoring them in counting the number of people required for congregational prayers, separating them from men during service, etc. The government has become an unwitting partner in such discrimination by making it easier for these institutions to raise funds.

The counter-argument would be that the desire of those women wanting gender equality within their faith must be balanced against the right of those who wish to follow the dictates of that faith even at the expense of their gender equality. Judges, aware of just such competing interests, generally do not like to prioritize among rights.

Stein, therefore, can vote with her feet, in two ways: abandon her faith altogether or move to a shul more respectful of her rights as a woman. But she does not want to do either. That, too, is her right—one that is being increasingly exercised by women of faith. As Zainah Anwar (2005) of the Malaysian Islamic feminist group Sisters in Islam, has written: "As believers we want to find liberation, truth and justice from within our faith." Or, as Amy Gutmann (2001, xxi), the noted American political scientist and philosopher, has put it in a different but still relevant context: "Oppressed women typically want their rights as individuals to be secured within their own culture, not at the expense of exile from their culture, or the destruction of what they and others take to be valuable about their culture."

Stein, then, has two further choices, that of conducting her campaign internally within her synagogue or, while remaining part of that congregation, taking the issue out into the public arena by mounting a Charter challenge. The legal action—or the mere threat of it, and with it the prospect of losing the charitable tax status—might prompt synagogues, churches, mosques and temples to find a theological way out of age-old patriarchy. History proves that scholars of most faiths can interpret religious texts to suit the occasion. I do not mean this derogatively but rather as a compliment. Divine or traditional texts may be immutable but their interpretation is human and hence ever-evolving. That's how faith practices change, generally for the better.

For example, in 2006, the Islamic Society of North America, the largest Muslim umbrella organization in Canada and the United States, elected its first woman president, Ingrid Mattson, a Canadian Catholic convert to Islam, now a professor at Hartford Seminary in Connecticut, who, as vice-president, had brought women's issues to the fore, including whether women can assume leadership roles.

Islamic traditionalists have long argued against electing or appointing women leaders. But the good news from the Muslim world is that centuries of anti-women rulings and interpretations are being swept aside, even while a great deal of cultural oppression of women remains. The four most populous Muslim nations—Indonesia, Pakistan, Bangladesh and Turkey—have already had women leaders, well ahead of Germany electing its first woman chancellor, the African continent choosing its first woman leader and the United States still awaiting its first woman president. The election of Mattson falls within this general reformist trend on gender equity in Islam.

Islamic feminists, like their Christian and Jewish counterparts, are rereading their scriptures "to demonstrate that the original texts are less misogynistic than they appear, and that alternative feminist readings have equal validity," writes British author Malise Ruthven (2000, 240).

I raise all this not to suggest patience, which Stein understandably has little of, but rather to illustrate that her campaign is timely and has resonance across faiths and geographical boundaries. The conversation she seeks is in tune with the times and, of course, long overdue.

I part company with her only to assert that the issue of gender equity in the faith communities in Canada—more specifically, the issue of bringing it into conformity with the Canadian Charter of Rights and Freedom—has little or nothing to do with multiculturalism. Religions that discriminate against women do so not in the name of multiculturalism but freedom of religion. The tension between the right to religion and the right to gender equality would exist with or without section 27 of the Charter, the interpretative multicultural clause. The issue will be ultimately resolved by the courts or Parliament, in the same manner that the courts have ruled that Indian treaty rights cannot be a cover for certain discriminatory practices against aboriginal women.

Separate Schools

The same tension exists when we consider the issue of religious schools. There are those, like Stein, who would question the validity of religious schools that meet general curriculum specifications but segregate women and girls in separate classrooms and, most particularly, during worship. This is a reference to Islamic schools. But I would argue that the Roman Catholic school system is a bigger culprit in this regard, for two reasons.

Unlike Islamic, Jewish and other private schools, Catholic schools in Ontario get state funding, up to Grade 12 (a policy justified—rather awkwardly, even by myself—in the name of living up to Canada's historic Catholic–Protestant compact, while similar funding to other religious schools is opposed for fear of diluting the public school system, the common Canadian cathedral for children of all faiths).

With their high enrolment levels, Catholic schools have a bigger reach than all other religious schools combined in influencing students not only on gender equality but also on abortion and gay rights, including same-sex marriage.

Therefore, the argument over religious schools running afoul of the Charter is not about multiculturalism but rather about a historic anomaly and, second, about the conflict between the right to religion and the right to gender equality and indeed other Charter rights.

Public Institutions

A similar conundrum hovers over the question of whether or not universities should make space available to student groups that segregate women in worship.

When a university bans such prayers, as has McGill with respect to Muslim group prayers, the issue is not multiculturalism but whether the institution is being punitive—or worse, selectively punitive—with people exercising their right to religion.

First, does a publicly funded institution not have an obligation to make, in the terminology of the courts and human rights tribunals, "reasonable accommodation" for religious practices?

Second, a university could not ban Muslim prayers but still allow a rabbi or a priest to bless the food or begin some formal proceedings with the Lord's Prayer. The tussle is, again, not over any multicultural imperative but rather over competing rights and, then, over the equal application of the law to all faith groups.

The Sharia in Canada

This tension also played out in the 2005–06 debate in Ontario about sharia law. Critics successfully turned it into a multiculturalism issue by mistakenly or dishonestly suggesting that the dreaded Islamic code of law was coming to Canada because Canadians are too accommodating of minority sensitivities.

Let's be clear: no sharia law could possibly have come to Canada, even if some of its proponents foolishly thought so and its critics gleefully echoed it ad nauseam while the media sensationalized it. Anyone implementing, or even threatening to implement, say, the provision for chopping off the hands of a thief would have faced prosecution under Canadian law.

Rather, the crux of the erroneously named sharia debate was Ontario's 1991 Arbitration Act — specifically, whether that law applied equally to all religions. Since Christians and Jews had been practising religiously informed arbitration in business disputes and such family matters as divorce and the distribution of marital assets, why not Muslims? It could not be credibly argued that Muslim women faced any more pressures to conform than women of other faiths. The Ontario government, therefore, had no choice but either to allow such arbitration for all faith groups or to allow none at all. It opted for the latter. Queen's Park thus came to the right decision, even if for the wrong reason (in response to the sharia hysteria), and in so doing, it answered Stein's central question: Does respect for different cultures extend to the sanctioning of religious courts that are likely to violate the rights of women? It did for fifteen years (1991 to 2006), with little or no public outrage, but it no longer did the moment Muslims entered the picture. The process was beneficial in two ways: we learned a great deal about latent anti-Islamism and we ended up ensuring the equal application of law for all religious groups.

Paradoxically, the government decision may have driven religious-based arbitration underground, thereby reducing public oversight over potential violations of the rights of vulnerable women, of all faiths. This is the conclusion of none other than Marion Boyd, former NDP attorney general of Ontario and a person of impeccable secular feminist credentials, who had been commissioned by the provincial Liberal government to conduct public consultations on the issue. There is a parallel here with the 2003 French law against the hijab in schools, which is also said to have had the effect of pushing young Muslim girls from religious families back into Islamic schools where they may not have the ability to interact with the wider community and where public oversight of their rights under French law may be reduced.

CONCERNS WITH MULTICULTURALISM

If the tensions about religious schools, public institutions and the possibility of using religiously based arbitrations in domestic disputes have little, if anything, to do with multiculturalism, exactly what sins should we be laying at multiculturalism's door? Terrorism? Increased violence in Canada? Threats to freedom of speech? The creation of ethnic ghettoes? Imbalances in income levels between native-born and foreign-born Canadians? Too much religion in the public square?

Before turning to each of these issues, it is important to reiterate that Canada has always been multicultural from an historical perspective, even if not legally so, until recently. The Canadian commitment to accommodate three distinct racial, religious and linguistic collectivities—the aboriginal peoples, the French and the English—was at the heart of the 1867 British North America Act. Today's multiculturalism is an inevitable extension of the same spirit, and carries with it similar challenges, only on a larger scale.

Terrorism

Since September 11, there has been some concern about "home-grown terrorism." It is suggested that rather than identifying with and being loyal to Canada, some Canadians may identify more with the lands of their birth or their ancestral homelands or, in the case of Muslims, with the *ummah*, the larger worldwide Muslim community.

But we have heard variations of such propositions before.

As constitutional scholar Alan Cairns of the University of British Columbia has written: "The pre-First World War debates between imperialist British Canadians and the rival liberal nationalists were about ... whether the boundaries of political community and civic allegiance were restricted to Canada or also, through ties of kinship and political tradition, encompassed the mother country"(1995, 157).

More specifically, worries over the extraterritorial loyalties of, and potential subversive activities by, some of our citizens also predate official multiculturalism.

During both the first and second World Wars, Ukrainian, Italian and Japanese Canadians were considered fifth columnists and interned. We, as a nation, have since apologized for those shameful decisions and, in some cases, paid reparations.

During the 1919 Winnipeg General Strike, Italian, Ukrainian and Jewish Canadians were accused of being Bolsheviks, plotting a revolution in Canada.

Following the founding of Israel in 1948, bigots at times accused Jewish Canadians of dual loyalty.

The flip side of such false accusations is the fact that some Canadians have indeed supported violent foreign causes, either by funding them or participating in them. But blame for such activities, too, does not rest with official multiculturalism, as we shall see.

Alleged Irish Canadian funding for the Irish Republican Army preceded the Multiculturalism Act, while Tamil Canadian financing of the Sri Lankan Tamil Tigers followed it.

The clearest case of home-grown terrorism—in fact, the biggest terrorist act ever concocted in Canada—was the 1985 bombing of an Air India jet, widely believed to have been carried out by militant Sikh Canadians angry at events in India. But we cannot credibly argue that the tragedy would not have happened had Canada not declared itself officially multicultural. A far more persuasive argument, based on official documents and court testimony, is that the tragedy could have been avoided had the Mounties and the agents of the Canadian Security Intelligence Agency (csis) not blown the leads that had come their way about highly suspicious activities by some Sikh militants in British Columbia.

Equally, multiculturalism has not hindered Ottawa in implementing sweeping security measures since September 11, policies that have had a deleterious effect on Canadian Muslims and Arabs, including Christian Arabs.

The Chrétien Liberals toughened the Immigration Act, gutted the Privacy Act as well as the Freedom of Information Act, and enacted the draconian Anti-Terrorism Act and the Public Safety Act, over the strong objections of lawyers, civil libertarians, human rights activists and journalists.

Similarly, Canada's multicultural imperatives did not prevent:

- the Maher Arar tragedy;
- the reported torture of three more Canadian Arabs in Syria, allegedly with Canadian complicity;
- the detention of five Canadian residents of Arab origins under so-called security certificates on secret evidence, a practice challenged, among others, by Human Rights Watch, before the Supreme Court of Canada, which has since ruled the practice unconstitutional;
- the 2003 mistaken arrest of twenty-three young Muslim men of Pakistani and Indian origins as "suspected terrorists," alleged members of an Al Qaeda sleeper cell, against whom not a single terrorism-related charge was proceeded with; and
- the summer 2006 arrest of eighteen Toronto-area Muslims on terrorism-related charges.

None of this is to say that some Muslims may not pose a security risk—only that we cannot blame multiculturalism for it.

To illustrate the point by contrast, recent Muslim acts of terrorism in the West—September 11, Madrid and London—occurred in nations that are not officially multicultural. That designation obviously does not make a whit of difference to the terrorists.

Still, given the fact that most terrorists these days are Muslims (in another era, they were Christian or Jews or Sikhs, and may in the future come from some other faith), some experts have speculated that Muslims may not integrate well into western democratic, liberal and non-violent societies because many have come from autocratic, oppressive and often violent societies. Under this hypothesis, the hundreds of thousands of immigrants who migrated from totalitarian communist states should not have integrated in the West. In fact, people from such origins are more likely to be appreciative of democracy than others who might take its freedoms for granted.

Even if one were to concede, for argument's sake, that Muslim immigrants may be prone to violence—because, say, "Islam is a violent religion," to invoke the populist parlance of the age—why it is that earlier generations of Muslim immigrants to North America and Europe did not produce terrorists? After all, Muslims have been around on both continents for more than 100 years, albeit not in the same numbers as now. The father of Mohammed Bouyeri, the murderer of Theo van Gogh in Amsterdam in 2004, was a guest worker from the Rif Mountains of the Maghreb, who was as unfamiliar with his son's "Islamic" extremism as others were in Holland.

To complicate the issue further, we are confronted with a darker reality: Bouyeri was born and raised in Holland, and the grisly note that he left behind at the scene of murder was written in Dutch, with a scattering of Arabic quotations; three of the four British bombers of the London subway were second-generation British citizens; the eighteen arrested Canadians are products of Canadian public schools and universities; and one of the British bombers and two of the charged Canadians are Christian converts to Islam, as was a Belgian suicide bomber who went to Iraq to conduct her evil mission. Like the friendly murderer from the neighbourhood who leaves everyone baffled, these young people left acquaintances and their mostly middle-class parents in a state of shock.

Not everything bad that Muslims do can be attributed to Islam, any more than Judaism can be blamed for some Jewish settlers committing violent acts against the Palestinians in the name of fulfilling their religious calling, or Christianity can be blamed for the Serbs invoking their faith in ethnically cleansing 200,000 to 250,000 Muslims in the former Yugoslavia.

Increasingly, security experts are attributing Muslim terrorism to the conflicts in Iraq, the occupied territories in Israel, Afghanistan and elsewhere, where tens of thousands of Muslims have been killed or maimed or oppressed. According to John Reid, the British home secretary, the official British report on the London subway bombings concluded that the culprits were "ordinary British citizens with little known history of extremist views," who were radicalized and motivated by "perceived injustices" committed by the West against Muslims (Hansard Parliamentary Debates 2006). A report by the Royal Institute of International Affairs (2005) also linked the bombings to British involvement in Iraq. Luc Portelance of csis, speaking of potential second- and third-generation Canadian terrorists, said: "Clearly, they are motivated by some of the things we see around the world (Siddiqui 2006b)." French academic Olivier Roy, an expert on Islam, said that "born-again Muslims," including converts, are following the path of European rebels of an early era: "Thirty years ago, a good many of them would have gone to the extreme left" to the Red Brigades or the Basque separatists (Siddiqui 2006c).

I bring up all this to illustrate that there are no easy answers, and that it is as facile to blame multiculturalism for the rise of a handful of terrorists in western societies as it is to lay collective guilt on all Muslims.

Hate and Violence

In multicultural Canada, are we too lax about expecting—indeed demanding—that leaders of religious and cultural communities take some responsibility when they hear members of their groups or congregations preaching the use of violence against others? Is there an onus on community leaders to speak up and to report dangerous views to the authorities? In posing the question in her essay, Stein quotes from a column of mine in *The Toronto Star*, in which I warned ("correctly," she says) against laying collective guilt on all Muslims, and argued ("incorrectly," she says) that "community leaders have no responsibility at all for what members do," as she paraphrased my contention.

That's not what I wrote. Instead, I raised the spectre of turning community leaders into vigilantes at a time when many Muslim organizations and individual Muslims are being damned, with little or no evidence, as terrorists or terrorist sympathizers. "Which self-appointed busybodies," I asked, "will use what yardstick to define 'a radical,' an 'extremist' or 'a Wahhabi'" (2006b)? These are some of the McCarthy-esque labels thrown at Muslims these days, sometimes by Muslims against other Muslims.

I went on to say:

> George W. Bush's first attorney-general, John Ashcroft, an openly Islamophobic Christian fundamentalist, proposed a program to ask Americans to snitch on fellow citizens. It was condemned as a totalitarian tool reminiscent of the old Communist states—and was dropped. Yet, here we are, suggesting about the same thing in Canada.... It is laudable that many Muslim leaders and groups are, voluntarily, offering to help in figuring out an early detection system to identify militant deviancy, especially among the young. But it is the responsibility of the state to ferret out and prosecute criminals, whether they invoke religion or not.

I stand by that democratic formulation.

Freedom of Speech

Does multiculturalism constrain freedom of expression? Is Canada drowning in multiculturally sanctioned political correctness, as some critics have alleged, citing the Danish cartoon controversy or, more specifically, the decision of mainstream Canadian media—newspapers as well as the national TV networks—not to show the controversial cartoons.

In commissioning and printing the caricatures of the Prophet Muhammad, the editors of the Copenhagen daily *Jyllands-Posten* invoked freedom of speech, of course, as did the handful of publications that reprinted the cartoons as an act of solidarity. But freedom of speech is not an unfettered right. It is circumscribed by laws of libel, hate and religious freedom, as Stein acknowledges: "[The law] does quite deliberately limit freedom of speech when that speech becomes hatred and incitement to violence."

In February 2006, notorious British historian David Irving was sentenced to three years for denying the Holocaust and radical British Muslim cleric Abu Hamza al-Masri was jailed for, among other things, inciting hatred. It was about time.

A few months earlier in France, the Catholic church won a lawsuit against a fashion designer who had depicted *The Last Supper* with semi-nude women instead of the apostles. The French case was clearly not of the same gravity as the British cases but it is relevant to our discussion, in that the French courts did curtail freedom of speech in the name of religious sensitivities.

Beyond the restrictions imposed by law, there is self-restraint.

PEN International, the writers' group that is the leading advocate of freedom of speech, speaks in its charter of the "unhampered transmission of thought," but it also insists that "since freedom implies voluntary restraint, members pledge themselves to oppose such evils of a free press as mendacious publication, deliberate falsehood and distortion of facts for political and personal ends." It calls on PEN chapters and individual members to foster "good understanding and mutual respect among nations ... to do their utmost to dispel race, class and national hatreds, and to champion the ideal of one humanity living in peace in the world."

Newspapers and magazines routinely reject cartoons that may be unfair or unnecessarily hurtful or racist. That's why we no longer see the caricatures of savage aboriginals, fat-lipped blacks, hook-nosed Jews or cross-eyed Chinese. That's our new multicultural sensitivity, if you will. That's why even *Jyllands-Posten* would not smear its pages with anti-Semitic graffiti, and that is precisely why it had rejected three years earlier a set of caricatures of Christ submitted to it by a freelance artist.

The lesson Muslims drew from the cartoon episode was that for many in the West, freedom of speech meant mostly the freedom to malign Muslims. This sentiment was summed up in a cartoon in the *Al-Quds al-Arabi*, the pan-Arab daily from London, showing an artist at work at *Jyllands-Posten*. In the first panel, he rejects a grotesque drawing of a black person: "This is racism." He rejects the second, which equates the Star of David with the swastika: "This is anti-Semitism." He keeps the longer third panel, of the Prophet's cartoons, saying: "This is freedom of speech."

Denmark has made no bones about its dislike of its Muslim population. In no European country is there so much xenophobia and hostility toward Muslims and Islam, according to the European Network Against Racism. Queen Margrethe has stated that there's "something scary" about the "totalitarianism that is part of Islam" (Olsen 2005). Prime Minister Anders Fogh Rasmussen's parliamentary coalition partner, the People's Party, has called Muslims "cancer cells," "seeds of weeds" and "a plague on Europe" (Siddiqui 2006a). The party also displays paranoia: "Muslim immigration is a way for Muslims to conquer us, just as they have done for the past 1,400 years" (Bilefsky 2005). "All countries in the West are infiltrated by Muslims. They are nice to us until they are enough to kill us" (Bilefsky 2006).

Jyllands-Posten is a populist paper catering to just such anti-immigrant and anti-Muslim prejudices. Here's Flemming Rose, the editor who commissioned the drawings, talking about Danish Muslims: "People are no longer willing to pay taxes to help support someone called Ali who comes from a country with a different language and culture that's 5,000 miles away" (Bilefsky 2006).

All this hate mongering cannot be divorced from the publication of the cartoons and how most Danes reacted to the controversy that followed.

Regardless of where you stand—worried over threats to freedom of speech or overt expressions of hatred toward an identifiable group or the West's blatant double standards—it is clear that multiculturalism was not a determining factor in the decision of most mainstream media across the West, especially in Britain, the United States and Canada, not to show the cartoons. Britain is only nominally multicultural, the US is decidedly against it and Canada is all for it, yet the media in all three cited the same reasons for taking a pass. As Edward Greenspon (2006), editor of *The Globe and Mail*, explained: "Here, at *The Globe and Mail*, along with the vast majority of newspapers in the Western world, the editors ... came to the conclusion that republication would be both gratuitous and unnecessarily provocative, especially given what we know about how offended Muslims, not just those in the streets but those counselling calm, felt about the cartoons.... Moreover, the arguments for publishing as an act of solidarity seemed somewhat bizarre given that the editors at *Jyllands-Posten* had expressed regret over their own decision to publish."

The Danish cartoon debate, along with the sharia debate in Canada as well as the polemic in Britain and Europe over Muslim women's hijab (head covering) and the niqab (the face veil), are all part of a growing cultural warfare waged by some people against Muslims and Islam. Rather than proffering these issues as examples of multicultural madness, we should see them for what they are: instances of post–September 11 paranoia that, regardless of whatever damage it causes Muslims, carries with it the danger of damaging our carefully crafted civil societies and diminishing our most fundamental democratic principles.

Immigrant Incomes

Recent immigrants to Canada are not doing as well as previous generations. Immigrants used to earn more, pay more taxes and own more homes than the native born. But, according to Statistics Canada, lately they haven't been, despite being the best-educated immigrants ever to arrive in Canada. There are also identifiable pockets of ethnic poverty, as shown in two separate studies in the Toronto area. However, these developments are not attributable to multiculturalism.

First, the level of education of the Canadian-born has gone up substantially; this means we no longer need, say, teachers from abroad, because we have enough of our own graduates.

Second, immigrants have been running into unusually high hurdles in having their credentials accepted by the nearly 400 self-governing regulatory agencies across Canada, partly due to racism, since two thirds of the newcomers are visible minorities, and partly due to Canadian unfamiliarity with the educational and other institutions in the countries most new immigrants are coming from, such as China and South Asia.

Third, the economic restructuring of the 1990s, due to free trade and globalization, including outsourcing, has dried up entry-level jobs in Canada, which immigrants typically used to accept as a stepping stone to a proper career.

Fourth, while the economy seems to require, at the high end, a highly specialized work force and, at the other, unskilled labour for the jobs that Canadians won't do, Ottawa seems incapable of matching immigrants to the needs of the market place; hence the phenomenon of PhDs driving cabs.

As real as these problems are—and by now well known enough to have forced several levels of governments and public agencies to work on potential solutions—they do not amount to what Stein calls "a sense of grievance" from which can grow "frustration, anger and, occasionally, an explosion of violence," such as the ones she cites, the 2005 youth riots in France and the smaller riots in England since 2001.

The problems faced by immigrants to Canada are nowhere near the catastrophic conditions confronted by immigrants in Europe, where too many have neither economic or social mobility nor acceptance as first-class citizens. Our immigration policy, as that of the United States, has historically been a citizenship policy, in that anyone who lives here lawfully for a prescribed period is entitled to citizenship and, therefore, full and equal rights.

We consider ourselves an immigrant nation and accept that we need more immigrants. But France and Germany—where the debate on multiculturalism is "louder, more strident," as Stein notes—each has a different self-image. Both nations live the myth that they are not immigrant societies, despite having had waves of immigrants in the twentieth century from across the continent as well as, in the case of Germany, from Turkey and, in the case of France, from the Maghreb.

Both nations also have a restrictive, indeed racist, notion of who is German and who is French. Even the British have, of late, had a debate over who is British. All these are manifestations of a question Canadians are familiar with: Who is a Québécois? Not the *pure laine* alone but anyone who lives legally in Quebec. Even the separatists have come around to that inescapable conclusion. All legal residents of Europe, therefore, are Europeans. Any other formulation will draw unflattering comparisons with autocratic oil-rich Arab states, which discriminate against expatriate guest workers and deny them citizenship.

Yet it was not until 2000 that Germany allowed Turks to take up citizenship, even though they had been residents for decades. In France, even those born in the country must pass an acculturation test at eighteen to determine suitability for citizenship based on knowledge of the French language and French culture. "If the Muslims say they pray regularly, officials take that as *prima facie* evidence that the applicants are not French enough and reject them," Professor Jytte Klausen of Brandeis University and author of *The Islamic Challenge: Politics and Religion in Western Europe* (Oxford: Oxford University Press, 2005) told me in an interview.

Whereas the cornerstone of the French model is that everyone living legally in France is French, regardless of religion or ethnicity, the children of immigrants, especially Muslims from North Africa, are not considered French precisely because of their religion and ethnicity. Unemployment among French Muslims is nearly double the national average of 9 percent. It is more than 30 percent in some of the *banlieus*, the crowded social housing projects outside Paris, the scene of the 2005 riots. Unemployment and underemployment extend to the second- and third-generation offspring of post–World War II immigrants.

In Germany, the jobless rate for German Turks is twice the national average of 11 percent. It is as high as 50 percent for younger Muslims in some cities.

French *laïcité*, the separation of state and religion, is another myth, because the state continues to provide hefty subsidies to Christian and Jewish separate schools. Germany, too, provides funding to both Catholic and Protestant churches, to the tune of €18.5 billion (in 2005). The Church of England is the state religion in Britain, even if as a hangover of history.

Given all of the above, why are we surprised that Europe remains, as Stein notes, "openly entangled in questions of how the 'other' can become the self, how the stranger can become less strange"?

Europe, mired in the toxic cesspool of xenophobia and Islamophobia, has little or nothing to teach Canada about how to attract and integrate immigrants.

"Ethnic Ghettoes"

Periodically concerns are raised about newcomers "segregating" themselves among their own religious, ethnic, cultural or linguistic groups. They are accused of attending their own houses of worship and not joining each other's religious celebrations, and sending their children to their own schools, their own summer camps, or their own soccer or hockey teams, with the result that by the time their offspring go to university, they tend to gravitate to ethnically or religiously based social clubs and organizations on campus.

The notion that there is anything new about this, or that it is a situation directly ascribable to multiculturalism, is fallacious. People of different faiths have always worshipped in their own churches; where else would they have done so? Few mainstream Christians ever "joined" the Jews for Hannukah in the good old days, any more than they helped the Eastern Orthodox celebrate their Christmas in January. Churches and synagogues have always run summer camps in this country. Religious clubs or sororities are not new to our universities either.

Students in Catholic schools have always stayed, and continue to stay, in their "community school" until their high school graduation. Students in Ukrainian-language schools in Alberta do the same. Do they—or students in exclusive private schools and, for that matter, in segregated boys' or girls' schools—turn out to be any less "Canadian" than those going through the public school system?

The phenomenon of "segregated communities," too, is as old as Canada. In *Strangers Within Our Gates*, a 1909 "study" for the Methodist Church in Winnipeg, J.S. Woodsworth—who later founded the Co-operative Commonwealth Federation, forerunner of the New Democratic Party—wondered about the ethnic ghettoes created by the heavy influx of Eastern Europeans and others, including "the Hebrews" and the Orientals ("Chinese, Japanese, Hindus").

He wrote:

> There is a very natural tendency for people of the same nationality to settle in large colonies. We have Mennonite, Doukhobor, Galician and Mormon colonies. Some contain 10,000 people in almost a solid block. Isolated from Canadian people, they are much slower to enter upon Canadian life. Such colonies are really bits of Russia or Austria or Germany transplanted to Canada.... They [are] less open to Canadian ideas.... The social, the educational, the religious, the political life is dominated by alien ideas. It would seem a wise policy to scatter the foreign communities among the Canadian, facilitating the process of assimilation.
>
> In the cities, even worse conditions prevail. Already we have the Chinese quarter and the Jewish or Italian settlements.

One finds echoes of this thinking in contemporary concerns about this or that ethnic enclave. In fact, a 2004 Statistics Canada study identified neighbourhoods across Canada with more than 30 percent of the population from a non-white ethnic group. Such communities, it said, had jumped from six in 1981 to 254 in 2001. About two thirds were Chinese. Bemoaning what it called the high "isolation index" of such communities, the study warned that "residential concentration of minority groups may result in social isolation and reduce minorities' incentives to acquire the host-country language or to gain work experience and educational qualifications" (Hou and Picot 2005).

I took strong exception to that conclusion and indeed the premise of the study. In a column entitled "Separation Anxiety," I asked several questions:

1 Socially isolated from whom? The mainstream, one presumes. But who, or what, constitutes the mainstream?

   Reached in Ottawa, Garnett Picot, one of the two authors of the study, said it is usually defined as "contacts between whites and non-whites." Really? In a city [Toronto] that's more than 50 percent non-white, non-contact with whites constitutes the defining measure of "isolation"?

2 Is there evidence that domicile in "minority neighbourhoods" reduces the residents' incentive to learn English or French?

   There's none, admits Picot.

3 Is there proof that people in such neighbourhoods are less likely to gain work experience? And what constitutes work experience? Does working in a Brampton Punjabi-owned business count? Or in a high-tech firm in Markham where the language of work is Cantonese?

   No, it doesn't, according to Picot.

4 Is there evidence that people in such enclaves are less likely to acquire education? What of all those Chinese and Asian students on our campuses? Do they all hail from outside the minority neighbourhoods?

   Don't know.

Picot says the study was merely recycling the assumptions found in academic literature, without any empirical evidence (Siddiqui 2004).

Senior officials at Statistics Canada have since given assurances that any further study along such lines will be more scientifically sound.

It is instructive that we don't fret over the concentration of Jews in Westmount in Montreal or the Italians in Woodbridge, or the Greeks along Danforth Avenue in Toronto, or the Anglo-Saxons in Rosedale in Toronto, if that indeed is its current "ethnic" mix. Why, then, the worry over Chinese Markham or Sikh Surrey?

I would argue that rather than being isolated, Canadians are closer to each other than ever before. Our urban centres are replete with vibrant ethnically mixed neighbourhoods. Take a walk with voter-savvy politicians who routinely hand out their calling cards in more than a dozen languages in their ridings. Canadians know each other far more than ever before—sampling each other's cuisine and culture, especially music; dating and marrying across racial and religious lines; and being actively involved in interfaith activities that have reached unprecedented levels. Critics of multiculturalism seem oblivious to this new, cosmopolitan and dynamic Canada.

Religion in the Public Space

Religion and politics have always been mixed in Canada, dating back to the British North America Act, which codified state funding for religious schools and linguistic guarantees for Catholic and Protestant minorities. The contemporary multi-faith environment has led to public policies that try to balance conflicting rights in our majority-Christian but not Christian country.

Human rights tribunals have held that employers ought to make reasonable accommodation for observant Jewish employees wanting to take Saturday off for the Sabbath. Most employers routinely let Muslim employees adjust their work schedules to take an hour or two off for the Friday noon prayers. Airlines, school boards and other public institutions have found compromises between the religious obligation of male Sikhs to wear the *kirpan*, or ceremonial dagger, on the one hand, and public safety on the other. Urban schools with a large non-Christian student body worry about how Christian the Christmas concert can be. Some draw the line at carols and the nativity scene. Others call it the winter concert, often combining it with a celebration of Hannukah or the Hindu festival of Diwali. This is the same tightrope walk that schools are doing in teaching nondiscrimination against gays and same-sex marriages without endorsing a lifestyle that many religious parents object to.

This has produced inconsistent results, for sure. There is no longer the reading of the Lord's Prayer in most schools but the Ontario legislature still opens its sessions with it. There's the Christmas tree in front of public buildings but not the menorah. Or there are both but not some other iconography—especially in Toronto where the majority of citizens are non-whites and non-Christian. But, overall, we have managed the evolutionary process better than the United States.

In fact, Canada, with a less rigid approach to the issue of church versus state has ended up with a more secular political culture than the US, which, despite its strict constitutional separation between church and state, finds its secular space increasingly breached by religion, as its politicians, Republicans and Democrats alike, pander to the 100-million-strong evangelical Christian constituency.

Limits to Diversity

Should there be limits, asks Stein, on "embedding diverse cultures and religious traditions within the Canadian context?" She notes that similar questions have been raised in England in the wake of the London subway bombings: "A new debate has erupted in London's magazines and salons about the limits to diversity that need to be put in place so that a culture of civil disagreement, rejection of violence and engaged citizenship can be created across the country's often segregated neighbourhoods."

The idea of "limits" to diversity or multiculturalism begins to crumble the moment you subject it to some simple questions.

Are we saying that we should limit the number of immigrants that we accept? Sovereign states already have that power, through formal or informal quotas. Refugee numbers are harder to control but not impossible, through narrower interpretations of the United Nations Convention relating to the Status of Refugees.

Or are we saying that people of certain cultures and faiths—Muslims, perhaps?—cannot come to our country? Or that they may but must check their culture or faith practices at the door? The latter is a new twist on the old bromide that immigrants had better develop amnesia the moment they set foot in Canada.

What we can and do demand of the new immigrants—something they accede to, anyway—is that they obey the law of their adopted land. They cannot import any cultural or religious practice that might run afoul of our law. Where there is ambiguity between the law and some egregious practice imported by some new immigrant group, the government moves to outlaw it, as Ottawa did with female genital mutilation, by amending the Criminal Code to remove any doubt about its illegality and to impose a stiffer penalty.

Some people's idea of limits refers to their desire to influence immigrant behaviour. They want newcomers to conform to some ill-defined standard. This wish sometimes takes the form of considering a code of conduct or a "social contract" for newcomers, as did Quebec in the early 1990s, only to abandon it in the face of public ridicule and legal limitations.

The law and the gamut of rules and regulations that flow from it already codify the limits of what people can or cannot do. The law, which is the ultimate expression of our shared values, is our holy parchment, the covenant by which we, both the foreign born and the native born, live.

The counterargument may be, as Stein says, that "the law will take us only so far." Indeed, the law does not regulate each and every component of our civil conduct—for instance, that we be polite to each other, stand in queues to take our turn, be respectful of each other's rights, do volunteer work in the community, and so on.

Even if such considerations could be catalogued, a seemingly inexhaustible undertaking, who should be entrusted with the task—a council of respected Canadians or some nongovernmental organization? But they would have no democratic legitimacy. Their recommendations would be no different than routine public campaigns exhorting citizens to, for example, keep their neighbourhoods clean. We might as well reduce our code of conduct to yet another pamphlet to be handed out to every arriving immigrant. But if the suggested code were to be given official approval by a government or a public agency, we would be back to the rule of law.

Another argument could be that the law is slow to catch up to the latest evil being imported by immigrants (although not always, as the case of female genital mutilation demonstrates). It is true that the law is generally slow in the making. That, in fact, is its strength. A hurried law is often a bad law. There may, therefore, be a gap between the manifestation of a problem and the eventual outlawing of it. But to worry about the delay only in the context of immigrants is clearly discriminatory. Letting self-appointed guardians of majority mores into such a void is to invite anarchy, and would be laughed off by the courts.

The answer to Stein's first question—Is respect for difference being polluted by a reluctance to set limits?—is simple: No. There is no reluctance; what we have instead is a deliberate decision not to set limits beyond those defined by the law.

The answer to her second question—How far can respect for difference go?—is the same: As far as the law allows, and no farther.

This is not a negative assertion. Rather, it is a stirring affirmation of one of the core beliefs of Canada: The strong shall not dictate to the weak what is, or is not, acceptable. That power rests only with the people's parliaments.

CONCLUSION

According to the United Nations, about 185 million people now live in countries other than those where they were born. Canada is in the forefront of this trend, being the most immigrant of western nations. While one in ten Americans is an immigrant, one in five Canadians is. Immigrants already provide 60 percent of our population growth; by 2020, they will supply 100 percent. Immigrants account for 70 percent of the growth in our labour force; they will account for 100 percent by 2011.

We invite immigrants not for altruistic reasons but because we need them. Without them, Canada would suffer a population decline and all the attendant economic woes.

Principally because of immigration patterns, Canada has also become one of the most urban nations in the world. Nearly 70 percent of Canadians live in cities, with 50 percent in just four urban centres—

the Greater Toronto Area, Vancouver, Montreal and the Calgary–
Edmonton corridor—and their surrounding suburbs, which are, in
fact, growing faster than the cities because of immigrants.

Whereas in previous generations, immigrants came to the cities
and then gravitated to the suburbs in the second or third generation,
today's immigrants are going to suburbs within the first generation.
This means that most of them are doing well economically, or bringing sizeable bank accounts with them into Canada. Whereas the defining feature of American suburbia is that it has been the refuge of the
whites, the Canadian suburbs are as diverse as the cities, and their
voting patterns are becoming about the same as those of the cities.

This trend towards the economic and social integration of our cities
and the suburbs is good news. Cities generate economic growth. Cities
also represent pluralism and cosmopolitan openness. Cities are where
the collective identity is the most fluid and evolving. The less fixed
that identity is, the easier it is for immigrants to fit in. No one need feel
marginal. No one's dignity need be trampled, in apt fulfillment of what
Charles Taylor of McGill University, one of our foremost philosophers,
described as the real aim of multiculturalism—extending equal dignity
to all groups. There is no one fixed culture, as Pierre Trudeau said;
every culture is equally valid, as long as it does not violate the rule of
law.

This bedrock Canadian principle, combined with the new breed
of highly educated and confident immigrants, has had a liberating effect on newcomers. They are not going to conform to our old-fash-
ioned notions of how immigrants should, or should not, behave. They
are not going to sacrifice their culture, religion and ethnicity, let alone
their sense of self-worth, to suit majoritarian mores. That Canada en-
ables them—in fact, encourages them—to be who they are is one of
Canada's core strengths.

This is not to say we have reached nirvana. Channelling a constant
flow of new immigrants into productive lives will always be a public
policy challenge, and in need of much discussion and debate. But our
national narrative on immigration and multiculturalism needs to be
more coherent and logical than it has been.

REFERENCES

Anwar, Zainah. 2005. "Islam and Women's Rights." Paper presented at the International Congress of Islamic Feminism, Barcelona, October 27–29.

Bilefsky, Dan. 2005. "Cartoons Ignite Cultural Combat in Denmark." *International Herald Tribune*, December 31, p. 1.

———. 2006. "Cartoon Dispute Prompts Identity Crisis for Liberal Denmark." *International Herald Tribune*, February 12, p. 22.

Cairns, Alan C. 1995. *Reconfigurations: Canadian Citizenship and Constitutional Change*, ed. Douglas E. Williams. Toronto: McClelland and Stewart.

Greenspon, Edward. 2006. "Self-censorship versus Editing." *Globe and Mail*, February 11, p. A2.

Gutmann, Amy. 2001. "Introduction." In Michael Ignatieff, K. Anthony Appiah, David Hollinger, Thomas Lacqueur and Diane Orentlicher, *Human Rights as Politics and Idolatry*. Princeton: Princeton University Press.

Hansard Parliamentary Debates (United Kingdom). 2006. "London Bombings," May 11, Column 520. http://www.publications.parliament.uk/pa/cm200506/cmhansrd/cmo60511/debtext/60511–0130.htm#06051139000959 (March 2007).

Hou, Feng, and Garnett Picot. 2004. "Visible Minority Neighbourhoods in Toronto, Montreal and Vancouver." *Canadian Social Trends*, Catalogue No. 11–008, Spring, pp. 8–13.

Olsen, Jan M. 2005. "Denmark's Queen Margrethe Says Religious Fanatics Must Be Resisted." Associated Press, April 15.

Royal Institute of International Affairs. "Security, Terrorism and the UK." isp/nsc Briefing Paper 05/01, Chatham House, 2005. http://www.chathamhouse.org.uk/pdf/research/niis/BPsecurity.pdf (February 2007).

Ruthven, Malise. 2000. *Islam in the World*. Oxford: Oxford University Press.

Siddiqui, Haroon. 2004. "Separation Anxiety." *Toronto Star*, March 11, p. A23.

———. 2006a. "Cartoon Furor Exposes Double Standards," *Toronto Star*, February 23, p. A25.

———. 2006b. "Muslim-Bashing Dilutes Our Democratic Values." *Toronto Star*, June 11, p. A17.

———. 2006c. "A Reality Check on Terrorism." *Toronto Star*, November 16, p. A31.

Let Sleeping Dogs Lie

John Ibbitson

Over the past few months, a new debate has emerged—a rather febrile debate, mostly confined to universities and the media—over whether there is a problem with Canadian multiculturalism. The problem is defined in different ways, but has a common element. Some Canadians, goes the argument, don't fully embrace Canadian values, as embodied in the Canadian Charter of Rights and Freedom. Their religions or their cultures contradict the values of equality, diversity and tolerance enshrined within the Charter.

Others suggest that the question is not one of the Charter versus multiculturalism—which is, after all, another of its values—but rather which Charter value should trump which. Is freedom of religion more important than free speech? Or equality? Or right of assembly?

Other contributors to this book know vastly more than do I about the philosophical and jurisprudential issues raised by, and imbedded within, the Charter. As a journalist and citizen, my principal concern is with the potential political impact of this debate on the street.

On that street, you will find many Canadians worried about multiculturalism, and about the country's open immigration policies. They don't talk about it in terms of the Charter; they talk about it terms of their own lives, and their own fears. They fear the country is losing its soul. We are taking in a million people and more every four years, from parts of the world that often have little or no common cause with secular liberal democracy. Because these immigrants may not share our culture of tolerance and equality, people fear, the rights of women could be at risk, and those of homosexuals and ethnic and religious minorities. Others, though they are very careful how they say it, worry that the European and Judeo-Christian underpinnings of Canadian society could be submerged beneath alien values brought in by alien races.

My position is simple: We should talk about the challenges of multiculturalism as much as we need to, both within and outside of the context of the Charter—and change nothing. The greatest risk we face is the risk of messing up a social formula that has proved remarkably successful, that could and should become a template for other societies. We should let the dogs sleep.[1]

SUCCESS! WE FAILED!

Why is Canada such a successful country? Simple: we are the product of a fortunate historical accident. In the late 1700s, once the dust had settled from the Seven Years' War and the American Revolution, the British found themselves with a unique problem in managing their remaining North American possessions. Apart from the aboriginal population, the territory consisted of a large and entrenched French colony in what used to be known as New France, alongside mostly British colonies in the Atlantic region, with yet more British, along with American loyalists, flooding into the wilderness to the west. British North America was evolving into a political space consisting of discrete French and British populations. It should have been a recipe for war, which is what the French and the British had been at, more on than off, in Europe since the Middle Ages.

The British solution—one the empire employed with varying degrees of success around the world—was to ignore the problem. The French in Lower Canada went their own way, under the watchful but mostly passive eye of an appointed governor, while Upper Canada, the Maritimes and Newfoundland did the same. The one attempt, in 1840, at uniting Upper and Lower Canada under responsible government was a miserable failure—the resulting assemblies were even more unstable than some of our recent Parliaments—and so in 1864 local politicians proposed dissolving that union and instead confederating the colonies into a collection of self-governing jurisdictions, with a general government charged with administering areas of joint concern. In that sense, Confederation was a divorce as much as a marriage: an agreement by the English and the French to create a minimalist state in which, as far as possible, each left the other alone.

It wasn't much of a recipe for nation building, but there was nothing for it. The chasm between British and French cultures made a Canadian nation impossible, despite the longings of editorialists and the best efforts of cultural reformers. However, the good news was that having no particular notion of nation meant that there was no precious culture to protect, which is one reason—filling an empty land was another—that Canadian governments encouraged immigration, with the general consent and approval of the population. We brought in waves of it, decade after decade: Irish and Germans, escaping famine and conquest; East Europeans and South Europeans, fleeing poverty and the wreckage of war; and, since the 1960s, immigrants and refugees from every part of the world who would rather be here than there. Today, roughly a quarter of our intake comes from China and environs, and a quarter from India and environs, with the rest hailing from the Caribbean, Latin America, the Middle East and Africa. We even take in a few from Europe, though not many want to leave there anymore.

We ask only of our immigrants that they embrace the principles of liberal democracy embodied by our governments and our Constitution—which are an amalgam of English and French political traditions—that they abide by the laws and accept the legal philosophy underpinning those laws—again, an amalgam of common law and civil code precepts—and that they respect the uniqueness of other peoples and cultures, just as others respect them, which is the essence of Canadian multiculturalism. The overwhelming majority of immigrants have had no difficulty living by these rules, because it was those rules, and the society that created those rules, that drew them here in the first place.

Sadly, this policy has done nothing to help unify Canada as a national entity; we remain as fractured and fractious as we were in the days of Brown and Cartier, King and Duplessis, Trudeau and Levesque.

It has, however, fitted Canada splendidly for its emerging role as the world's first truly cosmopolitan, post-national state.

THE NATION-STATE: SO LAST-CENTURY

Around the world, the curse of culture competing with nationhood bedevils most states. We continue to watch in despair as Africa struggles to overcome the caprice of colonial borders and corrupt and incompetent governments. Religious and racial faction tears at the states of the Middle East, destabilizes India and bedevils both the mainland and archipelagic states of southeast Asia. All of these countries have discovered that the ideal of the nation-state, in which the boundaries of a country are synonymous with the self-identifying nationhood of a people, is impossible to achieve and dangerous to attempt. People move around; identities are shaded, even contradictory; every state on the planet, it turns out, is multinational, like it or not.

This is even true of Europe, where the idea of nation-state was invented. Maybe the English are English and the Scots Scottish, but there was never a time when England was England, Ireland was Ireland, Scotland was Scotland and Wales was Wales. One way or another, they were always interlinked, and eventually became part of the United Kingdom, a multinational state if ever there was one.

Over on the Continent, things were even more complicated, with Germans in Poland and Hungarians in Romania and Hapsburgs ruling them everywhere. The French have always had a certain idea of France—though they hosted, and often oppressed, their own minorities—but Spain as a nation-state was problematic from the beginning; the Belgians, once they had wrested independence from the Dutch, promptly turned on each other; Germany and Italy, as nations, were initially unstable and belligerent, and the efforts of the victors after the First World War to carve up Europe along nation-state lines promptly set the continent on the path to the Second World War.

Whatever the European nation-state might have been, its complexion changed radically with the arrival of postwar immigration policies. For two generations now, the old countries have been, with varying degrees of reluctance, bringing in workers from foreign lands to supplement their dwindling populations, to infill the labour short-age for menial work and to salve their consciences. They have done everything wrong. First, they have obtained much—even most—of their intake from specific countries, often former colonies. Then they have consigned them to physical and cultural ghettoes, on the implicit understanding that you can bring people to Holland, but you can't make them Dutch. And then they have watched in horror as many of the children of these immigrants reject the home religion, the home culture and their assigned lot in life.

More often than not, this seething minority is Muslim, and dis-avows both the secular nature of European states and the Christian ethos that underpins their laws. Some observers—although the most extreme of them, such as Bruce Bawer, author of *While Europe Slept*, get rather hysterical about it—foresee the Lebanonization of Europe, with the continent evolving into pockets of white, Christian society and Islamic communities governed by sharia law.

Even the United States is not immune. Long afflicted with the legacy of slavery, Americans now confront as well the increasing His-panization of their society, with an estimated 450,000 Latinos pouring across the border each year, transforming the urban street, the labour market and domestic politics. It is quite exciting, in its own way, but also troubling for many of the descendants of European stock.

THE WORLD'S FIRST POST-NATIONAL STATE

Canada has escaped the worst of these problems. We bring in more people, per capita, than any place else on earth, and we do it the right way. We bring in Chinese and Indians, Bahamians and Egyptians, Poles and Paraguayans. The diversity of our intake ensures that we avoid creating a racial dichotomy: a white, European majority confronting a dominant racial, religious or culturally homogenous minority. Instead, the European majority is itself simply one of a swath of ethnicities, destined one day to become a visible minority of its own, thus ren-dering the term meaningless, as it already is in the largest cities.

Frankly, this shouldn't work. Our cities should be torn by ethnic unrest. Crime rates should spike, as unemployed young men driven by boredom and resentment over their exclusion look for quick fixes to poverty and lack of opportunity. There ought to be a right-wing political party championing traditional virtues and calling for an end to immigration. Race, language, religion, culture—these should all be fodder for enervating and divisive debate.

Instead, for the most part, we all seem to get along. We work together, party together, eat each other's food (and mix it up, in impromptu experiments with fusion cuisine), make love, get married, have babies, share neighbourhoods. We are enjoying the entrepreneurial and artistically creative energy that results from bringing a broad variety of cultural perspectives to problem solving, to making art, to selling goods abroad. Looking back at our bland, monocultural past—when you couldn't shop on Sundays, when the arts councils and the National Film Board funded unreadable novels and unwatchable movies, when everything Canadian on TV outside news and sports was execrable, when columnists made a perfectly good living running down the country three days a week: decrying our lack of identity, our inability to compete and the insufferable inferiority complex that seemed to define us—it's hard to deny that we now live in a healthier and more interesting Canada.

Yes, this is overly simplistic. Yes, it glosses over real problems. Not all communities are integrating successfully. Race-based crime is front-page news in Toronto and Vancouver and Montreal, though it does not begin to compare with that in many other North American and European cities. Militant Islam infects Canadian society too: at least one gang of young men, Canadian born, allegedly conspired to wage their own jihad by assaulting the Parliament buildings.

As Canada evolves into one of the world's most urban and diverse nations, its rural regions remain monochromatic and monocultural—cut off from the urban state of mind, their populations and economies generally in decline, and their citizens bewildered and resentful of the big cities that seem to have a monopoly on the attention and resources of government.

Far more worrying, generations of neglect and failed experiments have left Canada's aboriginal people—status and non-status Indians, Inuit and Métis—too often confined to isolation, poverty and exclusion.

This is not the place to analyze the causes of, and possible solutions to, this national disgrace. But it remains our most compelling and urgent dilemma.

Yet within a global context, Canada is comparatively the most peaceable of kingdoms, seemingly immune from the cultural stresses that are threatening the fabric of too many other states in both the developed and developing world. Not only immune—we are visibly thriving by pursuing the very policies that have led other countries into turmoil. So what's our secret?

Simply put, we owe our success as a country to our failure as a nation. To repeat: Canada never really had a chance to gel as a nation-state because the French and English divide was too pronounced. Even today, the great majority of English Canadians only dimly comprehend the Quebec dynamic. And though the Québécois are better acquainted with English culture, simply because it is so dominant, they often misunderstand Canadian society outside their own borders. You see it every day, in French and English newspapers and newscasts that offer profoundly contradictory analyses of current events, in public opinion polls that show French society holding opposing views to English society when considering world events (Quebec is less inclined to participate in overseas adventures, and is generally more sympathetic to underdogs that find themselves in conflict with the American colossus). You see it as well in French and English literature, in films (the French films are good; the English ones aren't), in the balance between promoting a market economy (the English preoccupation) and funding social programs (the French priority).

And we are not merely two solitudes. Atlantic Canada continues to protect and nurture the remnants of its Celtic inheritance and to exclude outsiders, which is one reason (though they won't admit it) why the Maritimes and Newfoundland take in far less than their proper share of immigrants each year. (Atlantic Canadians claim they can't bring in immigrants because their economies are too weak, as though the one weren't the product of the other.) The West, though a diverse region, continues in part to define itself as not being part of the East, and chafes at what many of its citizens believe is under-representation and funding from the federal government. Within the West, petro-wealth fuels an expanding and diversifying Alberta, the most American place in Canada, while British Columbia looks not east across the mountains but west to its Pacific markets. And Ontario, which once considered itself synonymous with the national interest, continues to evolve into a region of its own, preoccupied with the challenges of maintaining its manufacturing base and increasingly skeptical of the benefits that accrue from diverting its wealth to prop up the poorer parts of the federation.

Put it all together, and you have an atomized, alienated, disjointed gaggle of regions and peoples kept together for lack of any plausible alternative.

But if Canada never had what it took to make it as a nation-state, it became remarkably successful at being, not simply multinational, but actually post-national. It started, once again, with Quebec. Federal governments learned to tailor so-called national programs to specific Quebec demands, through compromise or simple submission to the minority culture's will, although mandarins and politicians preferred such euphemisms as opting out or asymmetricality. The ethos spread: governments at all levels became adept at, even fixated on, preventing the bulk of majoritarian sentiment from trampling on non-conforming minorities. (Provincial human rights codes were often more sweeping and more powerful than their federal equivalent.) This respect for the weaker "other" became a founding and guiding principle of the Charter of Rights and Freedoms, which may be the one unifying national symbol we have, since all but a few cranks accept and embrace its principles of equality and mutual respect.

Navdeep Singh Bains, the young Liberal member of Parliament representing Ontario's Mississauga–Brampton South, once explained to me the power of the Charter among minority cultures.[2] Bains was a strong supporter of same-sex marriage from the time it was introduced by the Chrétien government in 2003, even though many Sikhs and other South and East Asian immigrants in his riding were profoundly uncomfortable with the idea. I understand your discomfort, Bains told his constituents, but the rights of homosexuals are protected under the same Charter that protects your rights. If the Charter cannot protect gays, then it won't be able to protect you. He was comfortably re-elected.

In other words, our lack of national homogeneity, which has reduced Canada to a lowest common denominator of statehood, inculcated in the country an acceptance of diversity and a respect for minority sensibilities unmatched by any other place on the planet. Immigrants integrated more easily into the fabric of the society because the design of the garment was a mosaic, a patchwork quilt that welcomed and was enriched by new patches. And the absence of a dominant national culture made it easier to assimilate immigrants, since there was nothing all that intimidating for them to assimilate into.

Consider this hypothetical scenario: A young engineer has decided to emigrate from Manila and seek her fortune in a new land. For whatever reason, she has narrowed her search to two countries: Denmark and Canada. Copenhagen is a beautiful city, and Danish culture is rich. But our Filipino engineer will face considerable challenges if she moves there. First, she will have to learn Danish, one of the many European languages that has little currency outside its own borders. She will also have to accept that she will never truly be Danish. To be a Dane is to be the inheritor of centuries of history and cultural development. Danes act Danish, look Danish, think Danish. It isn't easy to be a Filipino-Dane. It may not be easy to be the grandchild of a Filipino-Dane.

But that same engineer, emigrating to Vancouver, faces a very different experience altogether. First of all, she probably has some rudimentary English—much of the planet does now—so it will be easier to make her way from the very beginning. Second, there will be plenty of other Filipinos to welcome her and provide a community in which she feels comfortable. Outside that community, she will find a city composed of Canadians of European heritage—most of them a melange of English, Celtic, German, Italian and who-knows-what-else—as well as large communities of East Asians and South Asians, along with the Latin American, Middle Eastern and assorted other diasporas. Almost all of them will welcome her arrival, just as they were welcomed when they arrived.

And she will find that we ask, on the one hand, much of her, but on the other, very little. She will see that she lives in a society built on an economy that encourages success and judges people in large measure by their ability to achieve it. There will be forms of social assistance for her if she needs it, but Vancouver in the early years of the 21st century — along with Calgary, Toronto, Montreal and most other cities — is a place that expects newcomers to make their way in this new world.

She will also discover that it is the easiest thing to feel Canadian, because it means so little. All she has to do is obey the laws, try to learn some of the words to the first verse of the national anthem and vote when she gets a chance. And she must try to get along with others, no matter who they are, just as others are expected to try to get along with her.

For critics, this is a recipe for disintegration. A Canada that is nothing more than a dormitory for ambitious migrants is not a real country, as someone might say. It has no soul, no ethos, no identity. No future.

In reality, it is a marvellous way to run a country. In fact, it's probably the way every country should be run. In that sense, Canada is a model for the world, a place that, to a greater degree than most others, has set aside ethnic conflicts based on national identity, in favour of a loosey-goosey multiculturalism based on individual opportunity and inter-group respect. Call it the post-national state. Some of us think it's quite wonderful.

DISCONTENTS

Opposition to Canada's policy of laissez-faire multiculturalism and open immigration traditionally takes one of three forms. Some critics argue that bringing in too many immigrants increases the labour supply, forcing down wages and impoverishing both immigrant and native-born workers. The argument has little currency among most Canadians, who recognize that the energy and upwardly mobile ambitions of immigrants benefit everyone.

A second argument is more nuanced. Immigration has benefited Canada in the past, goes this line of reasoning, because the Canadian economy has been able to absorb large numbers of unskilled workers. But the modern economy places a premium on skilled labour that can adapt and contribute to knowledge-based businesses. Because many new immigrants arrive speaking little or no English or French, because we bring in too many family-class immigrants who are older and less able to integrate into the labour market, and because federal and provincial governments spend too little on labour retraining while professional associations are reluctant to accept the credentials of foreign-trained professionals, immigrants today are more likely to start out poor and stay poor, increasing the risks of creating racially or culturally defined urban underclasses.

There is certainly truth to the argument that governments need to invest in labour and language training for new arrivals, and that the colleges of the professions should work harder at combating the inherent elitism of their members. And the balance of family-class versus economic-class immigrants should also be reviewed.

But with immigrants soon to be the sole source of labour-market growth in this country (and one day the sole source of population growth, too, but we'll get to that later), Canada would be taking grave risks by curtailing immigration. Labour shortages are emerging throughout the Canadian economy, as the baby-boom generation begins to retire even as that economy continues to expand. Fast-food franchises are having a hard time staying open in Calgary, as its overheated labour market promises high-school dropouts $20 an hour for just about any kind of job. When I was visiting Whitehorse in June 2006, a sign outside my hotel practically pleaded: "Now Hiring—All Positions." Labour shortages are rife throughout the Maritimes (although this may be more a sign of skewed Employment Insurance programs than proof that Moncton's economy is red hot). Now is hardly the time to be turning off the tap on the most important source of new workers available to us.

A new phenomenon is beginning to emerge in developed countries: remigration. As Asian economies—particularly the Chinese and Indian—continue to expand and modernize, immigrants here are increasingly tempted to return home, where family is waiting, incomes are now competitive and the food tastes better. Increasingly, national governments will have to compete for skilled immigrants, both with each other and with the Asian tigers, and will have to provide those immigrants with sufficient inducements to stay. Canada, with its robust tradition of integrating immigrants, and its large pool of settled immigrants available who can help make more recent arrivals feel at home, enjoys a strong advantage in this competition. It would be perverse to abandon that advantage by suddenly restricting the intake of new-comers.

There is another argument against immigration, one so discredited that it now is barely tolerable to raise it in public. Immigrants, goes this argument, are threatening the stability of this country because their values are alien. It was all right to bring in plenty of immigrants when those immigrants recognized and accepted the unwritten but implic-itly accepted tenets of Canadian culture, French or English. But new immigrants come from far more alien places. They're not like us. And the more we bring in, the more we threaten and endanger the social fabric that makes Canada such a success.

It is an ancient tirade that has been used by old stock against new stock for as long as Canada has existed. It was used against Irish Catholics, against Ukrainians and other east Europeans, against the Italians and the Portuguese and the Jews. It has long been used against the Chinese, but has recently been expanded to include those from the Caribbean, the Middle East, Africa, India. You can find it on some of the more loathsome websites, and it is regrettably present in a few Legion halls and curling clubs in smaller towns. It is false and it is racist, but it is there.

Lately, however, the most amazing thing has happened. The argu-ment has been reborn, not from its traditional home on the red-neck right, but from the very best salons of the left. It has the support of the most enlightened columnists, distinguished academics and talented politicians. It has been embraced by a British prime minister and other European politicians. It can be found in my own newspaper.

Let me rush to prevent offence. The motives and outlook of those making this new version of an ancient argument are entirely different from the resentful mutterings of the old stock. They are not seeking to preserve a Christian or European culture within Canadian society. They welcome the immigration and multicultural policies that make Canada such a delightful place in which to live today. But they have concerns.

They are worried that some immigrants are sinking into under-classes and that elements of these underclasses are violent. Although it is difficult to say, race-based gangs do plague some cities, and the men (for they are mostly men) in these gangs are the sons of immigrants from violent places, such as Jamaica. The fatal shooting of a young woman on Boxing Day 2005 in Toronto shocked the city because it happened right at Yonge and Dundas, and the victim was a young woman—who, yes, was white—caught in the crossfire when young black men began shooting at each other. So the question: Are we bringing in too many people from societies that have little experience with the rule of law? Should we be slowing down our intake from those countries?

And then there is the vexed question of Muslim immigration. Although many Muslim countries have, more or less, succeeded in creating secular governments—Turkey and Indonesia come to mind—others are largely theocratic extensions of a fundamentalist interpretation of the state religion. And even within secular Muslim states, many citizens live an orthodox, fundamentalist Muslim life.

Nothing wrong with that. But within the fundamentalist Muslim community, and its diaspora in Europe and North America, there are many—to borrow a word—evangelicals. They proselytize to the young, in particular, that Islam is not only a faith, but a way of life, a legal code and a system of government. Worse, they argue that the spiritual/legal/jurisdictional union of Islam is in conflict with western governments, secular values and all other faiths. A minority of young men and women, in London and Toronto as well as Amman and Tehran, have embraced this belief, and a minority of that minority have concluded that this justifies taking action against their own governments and fellow citizens.

The attacks on New York and Washington, subsequent terrorist outrages in Bali, Madrid and London, and the revelation of an alleged terrorist conspiracy in Canada have brought the problem home. Whatever the war on terror might be, the front line appears to be our own cities.

It has led to criticisms that otherwise might never have seen the light of print. Too many immigrants don't comprehend or fail to appreciate the tolerant, secular nature of Canadian society. Far, far worse, they do not accept the equality of women and sexual minorities in this society—a hard-fought struggle that is now enshrined in the Charter, in legislation and in landmark judicial rulings. There are rumours of female circumcision being carried out behind closed doors, of young women being forced into arranged marriages, of seething discontent over the open lifestyles of gays. No less a personage than British prime minister Tony Blair has called the niqab, the facial veil worn by some Muslim women, "a mark of separation."

There have been similar expressions of disquiet here at home. *Globe and Mail* columnist Margaret Wente (2006) described the niqab as "deeply alienating ... a powerful symbol of cultural separation and gender oppression.

"The trouble with the veil is not simply that it makes conversation difficult," she concluded. "It is that it stands for a set of behaviours and beliefs that are fundamentally incompatible with those of a liberal democracy."

Others, including my respected co-author Janice Gross Stein (2006), argue that when religious precepts conflict with the values underpinning Canadian civil society, especially as expressed through the Charter of Rights and Freedoms, we should debate the right of those religions to embrace those beliefs while also receiving tax concessions.

"We have to make explicit the contradictions between cultural and religious traditions and the rule of law in Canada, when such contradictions exist," she wrote. While we must always seek to achieve balance, "if we cannot find that balance ... we need to make clear that the conflict is real and serious."

And then there is the anecdotal evidence: the conversations around dinner tables, the debates within the newsroom, the talking heads on television. A good friend who is both a feminist and a lesbian confessed recently that the sight of a woman wearing a hijab makes her deeply uncomfortable. It stands, for her, as a repudiation of decades of struggle for gender equality. And if it is acceptable for women to publicly express submission—not to God, but to men—then how long will it be before the hard-fought rights of homosexuals to live in peace come, once again, under attack?

These are not the grumblings of old men who lament that things aren't the way they used to be. These are the expressions of concern by deeply thoughtful people who fear that an obsession with political correctness and the growth of what Stein calls "shallow multicultur- alism" — communities living side by side in isolation — could lead to social unrest and the loss of the very tolerance that is the bedrock of true cultural diversity.

Yet, while we must debate these concerns — we must debate every concern, every time, for debate is the lifeblood of public discourse — we must also be careful. The travails of Prohibition came about because social reformers found themselves in common cause with religious zealots, forming a dangerously powerful coalition that, in the interest of improving society, forced an unwelcome law on the population that led only to organized crime and bad gin. In more recent times, social activists and conservative Christians united in the fight against pornog- raphy, while pacifists and isolationists have made common cause in re- fusing to confront challenges from abroad.

Such coalitions invariably seek to limit freedoms in the name of justice, which is always a dangerous path to walk.

That is one reason why many of us so strenuously oppose those who, with the best of intentions, seek to redefine the civil obligations of Canadians within the context of the Charter, religion and public conduct. But there are other reasons as well.

THE VEIL AND THE GAY LEATHERMAN

The best riposte to Margaret Wente's column on the veil came from Paul G. Leroux (2006), who sent in a letter to the editor.

"As a gay leatherman, I understand how one's dress proclaims a set of underlying values," he wrote. "It is unfair to single out Muslim women for criticism when other groups distinguish themselves by their outward appearances and seem to reject modern Western ways. Think of the Amish or Hasidic Jews. Do we tell them, 'If you don't like living here and don't want to integrate, then what the hell are you doing here?'"

He concluded: "The fact that Muslim women choose to live in Canada indicates their desire for inclusion. But, like a leatherman's gear, their mode of dress says, 'I want to add to the diversity of Canada's

their impoverished homeland, their children would chafe at being excluded from full participation in the life and economy of the host country. This is why the Europeans are having such agonized debates about citizenship and multiculturalism and whether the hijab should be allowed in the schoolyard and whether people in Holland should be required to pray only in Dutch.

But we don't need to have this debate. Canada's policy of recruiting immigrants from all regions of the world reduces the danger of creating a single large, ethnically or culturally homogenous underclass. Only about 2 percent of the Canadian population is Muslim, and there is no reason to believe it will ever get that much higher. Europe may be worrying about turning into Eurabia, but Canabia isn't ever likely to happen.

For another thing, there isn't any reason to believe that large numbers of native-born Muslims are turning away from Canadian society. There is no reason why they should. To repeat: unlike Europe, Canada has a strong tradition of welcoming new immigrants, and the lack of an entrenched culture makes it far less likely that Muslim youths here will grow up feeling alienated and victimized. The only ones who feel that way have other, larger, problems.

So it is wrong to say that political correctness, or a desire not to offend, is keeping us from facing a growing threat. There is no threat, pure and simple.

That does not mean that there aren't some troublemakers within the immigrant community. There always have been, whether they were Irish toughs or Italian Mafia or the Chinese tongs. New arrivals are vulnerable, and some members of their own community prey on that vulnerability. And yes, there is clear evidence that a few young Muslims are not integrating and are listening to dangerous messages. It only takes a small cell of well-trained martyrs to wreak havoc.

But we have tools to deal with this. We have laws to guard against dangerous speech, and laws to guard against terrorists, and police and security services with both the mandate and the resources to keep a close watch. So far, they seem to be doing a pretty good job. If anything, the case of Maher Arar suggests that the problem is not one of lack of vigilance, but of overzealousness.

Most importantly, we have a Charter, which protects the rights of all, and we have courts to interpret that Charter, when rights come in conflict.

The biggest problem with the argument against toleration of cultures and religions that conflict with Charter rights, or that bring one Charter right into conflict with another, is that we really don't know what is being proposed by the people who make this argument. They speak of the need for debate and dialogue and they speak of difficulties and discomfort, but they never actually come out and say what it is they want done. This is very frustrating for the rest of us. You can insult a Muslim woman by telling her that her dress makes you uncomfortable, but apart from being rude, what have you achieved? You can talk about bringing the Charter inside the church, but apart from uniting rabbis, priests, imams, preachers and libertarian atheists in common cause against you (which may not be such a bad thing), what do you hope to accomplish?

Every now and then, as part of this debate, someone will argue for a renewed definition of citizenship—a reaffirmation of the social contract—so that those arriving here, or those born here of immigrant parents, know exactly what is expected of them in this society.

But, again, what does that mean? A new loyalty oath? An expanded definition of citizenship? Or worse, a qualified citizenship that puts new arrivals on some form of probation until they have proven they can fit in?

Whatever it is, some of us are ready to oppose it. We'll fight tooth and nail. Why? Because we already have a Charter. We already have laws, and no one has put forward a decent argument that they are insufficient.

All this ideological shadow-boxing is aggravating, because no one has yet come forward with a concrete proposition: a piece of legislation, an amendment to the Charter, a new oath of citizenship.

Maybe people are reluctant to get specific because they know most of us would find their proposal anathema.

IT'S A GETTING-SMALLER WORLD AFTER ALL

In about three decades, maybe four, the global population will cease to expand and start to shrink. India, China, Brazil, Indonesia are all either at, near or below the fertility rate of 2.1 children per woman needed to maintain current population levels. The population of some developed countries has already started to decline. The United States will continue to grow, albeit slowly, thanks to high Latino birth rates (although those rates will soon decline as well). Canada should be able to keep its population stable over the long term through immigration. For most developed countries, that is the only choice: bring in more immigrants, or get smaller. Japan, which permits virtually no immigration and has a low birth rate, is already shedding population.

In this context, arguments about restricting immigration are nonsensical. We can imagine the day when that engineer in Manila posts a web announcement declaring that she wishes to emigrate, and countries around the world send lucrative proposals. First year free rent! Instant certification! And then, in the end, she will stay, because the best offer of all will come from the government of the Philippines.

So before we start offending Canada's immigrant community by insulting their choice of clothing, by questioning their loyalty, by demanding that they be more, well, *something,* let's remember: Those immigrants are our future, our best and only hope of renewing ourselves. But then, they always were.

It is Magna Carta. It is the Bill of Rights. It is the Charter of Rights and Freedoms. The state shall not constrain the liberty of the citizen except in specific instances governed by law, approved by a majority of the population and judged legitimate by the judiciary. Democracy is about limited government. All other forms of government are about government without limits.

That is the last and most potent reason for doing nothing. The Charter is in place. The principles and policies of multiculturalism are in place. So what more is needed? When the question of doing something or doing nothing arises, in whatever context, the answer must always be to do nothing, unless the reason for doing something is compelling. That is what limited government is all about.

So let women dress as they like. Let men and women arrange their families as they see fit, and worship as they see fit, and live their lives as they see fit, whether they be immigrant or native-born, Christian or Muslim, gay or straight.

And if somebody out there wants to change all that, to change the definition of citizenship or to limit religious freedom or to define approved conduct, well, we'd like to hear exactly what it is they are proposing, in clear and unambiguous language. And we would like to warn them in advance that we suspect most people won't approve. Most people probably won't approve big time.

That's why we should let the dogs sleep. Waking them up will only create a lot of barking and ill will.

And, before we are anything else, let us be people of good will.

NOTES

1 Some of the arguments in this chapter are drawn from previous writings, in particular *The Polite Revolution: Perfecting the Canadian Dream* (Toronto: McClelland and Stewart, 2005); "Citizen-Centred Federalism: An Alternative View," *Managing the Federation: A Citizen-Centred Approach* (Ottawa: Crossing Boundaries National Council, 2006); an address given at the University of Prince Edward Island in August 2006; and columns in *The Globe and Mail*.

2 Taken from a conversation with the author.

REFERENCES

Leroux, Paul G. 2006. "Beyond the Veil." *Globe and Mail*, October 14, p. A22.

Stein, Janice Gross. 2006. "Living Better Multiculturally." *Literary Review of Canada*, vol. 14, no. 7, pp. 3–5.

Wente, Margaret. 2006. "Let's Raise the Veil on Veils." *Globe and Mail*, October 12, p. A23.

An Evolutionary Story

David Robertson Cameron

Canadians are often charged with being nice. And accused of being smug. Frankly, I don't mind the first label, but I don't want to be told I am smug.

Let me take that risk, however, by saying that there is a widely held view—and not just within Canada—that this country has done a pretty good job of managing diversity. Not perfect by any means, but, in comparison to most other countries, creditable. I believe this to be true. In Canada, social exclusion does not correlate too closely with immigration patterns. Our cities, which are where the vast majority of our recent immigrants locate, are safe and fairly peaceful by international standards, and there are relatively few ethnocultural no-go zones where other citizens and residents feel unwelcome or threatened. People from all over the globe appear to believe that, in coming here, they and their children will have a pretty good shot at the Canadian dream—although, perhaps significantly, none of us is entirely clear what the Canadian dream is. There is virtually no political voice arguing that we need to staunch the flow of immigration to increase our national security. Indeed, rightly or wrongly, we do not as a nation feel particularly insecure. So far, we have not been seriously exposed to the kind of home-grown explosions of anger and violence that have been associated with multiculturalism in societies elsewhere.

Consider the reaction of Canadians to the alleged terrorist plot that came to light with the arrest in Toronto of seventeen people in June 2006. Far from dominating political discourse in Canada in the months that followed, this event sank virtually without trace from public view. One might contend that public perceptions of the gormlessness of the Royal Canadian Mounted Police (RCMP) and the Canadian Security Intelligence Service (CSIS) plus the amateurish conduct of the suspected conspirators might explain the low-key reaction of Canadians, but, even taking that into account, I suspect that an event such as this would have triggered very different reactions in the United States, in the United Kingdom or in France. That is partly because of the difficult experiences with terrorism and inter-communal conflict those countries have suffered in recent years; indeed, if Al Qaeda were to make good on its threat to launch a terrorist attack against Canada in punishment for our participation in the Afghan war, we might end up looking and acting quite a lot like other western countries.

The distinctive Canadian reaction, however, may be partly because the situation of ethnocultural minorities in those countries is somewhat different than it is in Canada. Canada's patterns of immigration and its experience with cultural pluralism may have led to somewhat less exclusion of minority communities from the mainstream of Canadian life. The reaction of Canada's Muslim community to the June 2006 arrests was very temperate and responsible: urging calm, accepting the possibility that the charges were true, considering the responsibilities of their leaders vis-à-vis Muslim youth, acknowledging that *if* the charges were true those accused merit prosecution. While there were understandable fears about a backlash, and worries about the accuracy of the information on which the raid and arrests were based, there appears to have been a general willingness on the part of much of the Muslim leadership to let justice take its course. Among Canadians in general, there was no hysteria and a very moderate, common-sense reaction to these events, in some ways paralleling that of the members of the Muslim community. There seems to have been little inclination to scapegoat the Muslim minority or to assume its disloyalty or untrustworthiness.

Multiculturalism—a term typically used to describe the ethnocultural diversity arising out of immigration together with the public policies designed to accommodate it—is, properly speaking, a subset of the broader concept of cultural pluralism. French and English migration to what is now Canada during the 17th, 18th and early 19th centuries is not normally thought of as immigration, except by Native people, who joke ruefully that their main problem back then was that they did not have a good immigration policy. The co-habitation of aboriginal and European peoples and the subsequent coexistence of the French and English were the earliest forms of cultural pluralism this part of the world experienced. The first has been largely ignored until very recently, and our experience with the second, I would argue, set the stage for our successful management of the third form of cultural pluralism—namely, multiculturalism—when it arose, most forcefully after the Second World War.

Canada's monumental failing in the management of diversity does not usually get discussed under the heading of multiculturalism, yet any comprehensive understanding of the pluralism of cultures in the Canadian context would have to include the country's relations with indigenous peoples, and here the historical record is a sorry one. We have failed miserably in finding the means of living honourably with aboriginal people. When, in the mid 1980s, Glenn Babb, South Africa's combative ambassador to Canada, compared the position of Native Canadians on reserves to the position of blacks under apartheid, the accusation stung because there was more than a little truth in it. While there has been significant progress in Canada since the 1980s, a review of relative poverty, mortality, incarceration, and drug and alcohol rates should be enough to persuade even the most skeptical that this is not a part of our national life of which we can be proud. My focus in this essay, however, is not on the fortunes of indigenous peoples, but on the terms of association among Canada's immigrant communities, within which I include for the purposes of this discussion the French and the British.

TWO SOCIETIES AND MULTIPLE CULTURES

My effort to understand will take us back into the past—perhaps surprisingly, back to Lord Durham, and his analysis of what is surely the most profound manifestation of cultural pluralism in our country, the coexistence of Canada's two great linguistic communities.[1]

The discussion of Canadian multiculturalism is very often carried on without much reference to Canadian historical experience, yet it seems important to me to appreciate the fact that Canada has wrestled with, and has been profoundly shaped by cultural pluralism since its inception. Indeed, from its very beginnings, British North America was deeply marked by challenges relating to the reconciliation of different cultures. The divide between European settlers and aboriginal peoples was effectively extruded from the body politic; once the power equation had altered definitively in favour of Europeans, aboriginal people were effectively pushed aside and ignored.

That approach was not so easy when it came to the ethnocultural division between the French and the British in British North America. The defeat of the French on the Plains of Abraham in 1759 left behind a vexatious problem for British policy makers. While a few of the inhabitants of New France left the country, the vast majority did not. A flourishing French, Roman Catholic community of some 60,000 souls, spread along the banks of the St. Lawrence River, came into the possession of Great Britain, and the policy question was what to do about it. Given their numbers, deportation did not appear to be a feasible option, as it was deemed to be for the Acadians who were expelled from the East Coast. The early decades of British North America were marked by an unresolved debate between the relative merits of accommodation and assimilation, but, while the debate was going on, events on the ground were pushing inexorably in the direction of accommodation. Even after the Constitutional Act of 1791, however, which pretty definitively set out the terms on which a French Canadian community would be tolerated in British North America, the evidence of a residual desire to follow the other course is evident in the government letters and the state papers of the era. The toleration of French Canada, and of its language and religion, meant that a cultural dualism was embedded in the very structure of British North American society, and the tensions it wrought are apparent in the history of the early years of the 19th century, tensions that played a significant role in the Rebellions of 1837, at least in Lower Canada.

In the aftermath of the '37 Rebellions, Lord Durham was sent out from London to report on what was wrong and how to fix it. He was one of Britain's most advanced social and political thinkers, a liberal whose radicalism was discomfiting even to many of his allies. He was also an enthusiastic British imperialist who saw the hand of God and destiny in the ultimate domination of the entire North American continent by the English people, "the great race which must, in the lapse of no long period of time, be predominant over the whole North American Continent" (Durham 1982, 146). Hardly a reassuring point of view for the French community that had inhabited the banks of the St. Lawrence for more than a century by the time he paid them a visit. With a candour characteristic of an earlier age, Lord Durham launched a merciless and scathing attack on the French Canadians, who clung "to ancient prejudices, ancient customs and ancient laws, not from any strong sense of their beneficial effects, but with the unreasoning tenacity of an uneducated and unprogressive people" (28). Retaining "their peculiar language and manners" (150), they were a people with no history and no literature, "an old and stationary society, in a new and progressive world" (28). These powerful declarative statements have echoed down the years on both sides of the language divide, shaping prejudices and perceptions through the generations. Small wonder that French-speaking Canadians have customarily remembered Durham for his English ethnocentrism, not for his liberalism, and have regarded him warily as a kind of bull terrier of the British imperial establishment.

Yet these two convictions, namely, the belief in the superiority and mission of the English race and the commitment to the progress of liberty in the world, coexisted without apparent difficulty in Durham's mind and received synthetic expression in the pages of his report.

Living, as we do, in a more relativistic and culturally sensitive age, we find Lord Durham's comfortable reconciliation of liberalism, cultural superiority and empire to be a good deal more problematic than he did, and his confident assertion that God Himself had had a hand in establishing the dominion of the English-speaking people in North America more a rationalization than an argument. But anyone who consults the political literature of Victorian England will be aware that Lord Durham was far from unusual in holding this combination of opinions. He is squarely in the John Stuart Mill camp in believing in the incompatibility between cultural pluralism and liberty. "Free institutions," Mill (1958, 287) wrote, "are next to impossible in a country made up of different nationalities." The diversity that Mill so avidly sought in his liberal philosophy was a diversity of belief and ideas, not a diversity of ethnic origin, language or culture.

Lord Durham's response to his finding that there were two nations warring within the bosom of a single state was a set of recommendations designed to offer resolution by dissolution: he resolved the problem by seeking to dissolve one nation into another. He did this in the fond belief that, like the Acadians of Louisiana, French Canadians would be the better for it; they would give up most of the active features of their nationality and, in return, would receive the opportunity of full and equal participation in the life and affairs of British North America. His object in uniting the two Canadas was to compose Lower Canadian society and its power structure differently; with continuing British immigration into a new, united province, the French Canadians would eventually be swamped by the English in a constitutional order they did not control; in time, they would begin to participate in the English system of economic progress and political liberty, and would resign themselves to their gradual disappearance as a national community.

The troubles that brought Lord Durham to Lower Canada were social and cultural in character and went to the core, not only of British North America's relatively brief history, but of whatever future it could construct for itself as well. That Durham saw the character and seriousness of the crisis is evident in his observation that a response that left the elements of society unaltered would fail. The relatively simple introduction of limited representative government in the other colonies would be sufficient to relieve the tensions there, but in Lower Canada that would not suffice. He saw the seriousness of the crisis clearly, but did not appreciate that it was, in fact, too serious—too structural—in its character to be successfully addressed by the means he suggested. The line dividing English and French was as primordial in the social geology of British North America in 1839 as it is in Canada today. If the society forming itself on the northern half of the continent were to crack, it would crack along that line. The point, then and now, is not to make futile efforts to erase the fault line, but to learn to live with it, and to render the social and political institutions of the country, as far as possible, earthquake-proof. The relationship between the French and the English in North America is, finally, not a problem at all, but an existential reality to be acknowledged and accommodated, one that has spawned a slew of problems, admittedly, but that has been too intimately related to existence and identity to be considered a "problem" susceptible to "resolution"—in the way, for example, that 19th-century Canada's problem with its large size and small population was solved by immigration and the construction of a national railway system.

Insensitive to the power and durability of culture and nationality, Lord Durham found French Canada grievously wanting and, therefore, of relatively little account. He allowed his analysis to lead him to a flawed conclusion, namely, that a society that he judged to be backward was therefore weak and without significant defence, and could be dismantled through peaceful and political means. He did not realize that that territory would not be won easily, if at all.

Indeed, it was the very effort to combine political liberty and cultural assimilation that was doomed to failure. A sufficient exercise of power may well keep the national sentiments of a subject people in check, at least for a time. However, in the absence of that power, and in fact with the specific intent of establishing government based on consent, the notion that a numerically powerful minority could be assimilated through constitutional means—at least in the context of British North America—was doubtful in the extreme. The point was not that a free society was impossible without assimilation, but that, in Canada at least, it was impossible with it.

Not Mill and not Durham, but Lord Acton was the thinker who provided the intellectual foundation for the direction that British North America—despite Durham's Report—was already destined to take. Another Victorian liberal as famous in his own day as Durham and

Mill, Acton (1964, 185), in a celebrated essay, wrote: "The co-existence of several nations under the same State is a test, as well as the best security of its freedom. It is also one of the chief instruments of civilisation ... and indicates a state of greater advancement than the national unity which is the ideal of modern liberalism." The course British North America was set upon was not the suppression of one national community but the mutual accommodation of two, a development that was ultimately to play a key role in Canada's emergence as perhaps the world's most advanced multicultural country.

It would be quite inaccurate to imply that the evolution of Canada in this way was the expression of some explicit collective preference. It was more a matter of circumstance than volition. The capacity of the colonies scattered along the northern edge of the United States to do otherwise than they did was ultimately recognized to be fairly limited. The mutual accommodation of French and English, then, was a necessity and, for many, a regrettable necessity. One might characterize a good deal of the history of French–English relations since that time as an attempt to make a virtue of necessity.

And a virtue we have made it. It has taken generations to reach this understanding, but Canadians have learned that Canada must be understood as a country composed of two language communities, or it will not exist. In the school of cultural pluralism, this is, surely, the toughest and most fundamental lesson we have learned, and I would argue that it has provided the platform on which we have constructed our contemporary practices and understandings in the area of multiculturalism. Had we not been forced to struggle, since our very beginnings, with the existential reality of cultural dualism, we would not have been nearly so well equipped to adapt ourselves and our society to cultural pluralism. Clearly, dualism and pluralism have been on many occasions in competition with one another, but with the "pluralizing" of Québécois identity that has occurred during the last couple of decades, multiculturalism has been integrated into the understanding that both language communities have of themselves. Thus we now have multiculturalism imprinted on Canada's two linguistic societies. Multiculturalism has become an architectural feature of the Canadian reality that is almost as deeply ingrained in our collective existence as is the dualism between French and English.

DUALISM TRANSFORMED

It is worth noting that dualism itself has changed substantially over the generations. For more than a century after Lord Durham wrote, the terms of settlement were defined essentially by the coexistence of what might be called mutually compatible solitudes. This meant that, on the French Canadian side, the social and economic circumstances were not much different from what Durham had predicted in the absence of assimilation: the agrarian idyll of parish, family and farm. The character and values of French Canadian society were sufficiently different from those of English Canada that the scope for direct conflict and competition between the two was more restricted than it otherwise would have been. Grossly oversimplified, the English could get on with commerce and industry in the cities, and the westward expansion of Canada, if the French were prepared to satisfy themselves with a substantially agrarian lifestyle on the banks of the St. Lawrence, protecting their language, their faith and their distinctive culture by standing apart as much as possible from the forces transforming 19th-century North America. Clearly, it was not ideology or culture, but circumstance and necessity that tied French and English together.

After World War II, social and economic forces, which had been at work throughout the century, pushed Quebec toward the adoption of a new collective cultural strategy that brought the two linguistic communities much more directly into competition with one another. From a condition of mutually compatible solitudes, we moved to a condition in which the aspirations of Quebec came directly into conflict with the English minority of the province and the assumptions of the rest of the country, largely because the Québécois began to want the same things. As French Quebec's values and aspirations became more like those of English Canada, so conflict between the two societies deepened. It became a zero-sum game, for what the Québécois sought necessarily involved the denial of the practices, assumptions and prerogatives that English Quebec had enjoyed for generations. Bill 101, Quebec's language law, perfectly illustrates this; if French were to advance in Quebec, English had to be made to retreat. Quebeckers in fact have become the modern, secular, commercial, bustling society that Lord Durham thought they were incapable of, but they have done it *en français* and collectively, not by assimilation.

The challenges from Quebec during this period contributed to the remarkable transformation of English-speaking Canadian thinking about national identity. Even after the Second World War, it would have been common ground for anglophones to think of Canada as a white, Anglo-Saxon Protestant (wasp), English-speaking country, closely connected to the "old country" by ties of loyalty, sentiment, language and shared historical experience. It was also understood to be a country with a large French, Catholic minority within its borders, in which it was understood that it was up to the French minority to learn the language of the majority, even in Quebec where the numbers told a different story. Today, the ties to England are gone, as are the assumptions of waspness, and English-speaking Canadians now see themselves inhabiting a country composed of two linguistic communities with two official languages. Generations of English-speaking schoolchildren in French immersion programs attest to that fact.

So the challenge of accommodating the new Quebec was one of the major forces leading to the transformation of English-speaking Canada. The other force, also a postwar phenomenon, was immigration, which added multiculturalism to the English-speaking Canadian understanding of national identity.

Somewhat later—and partially as a result of Bill 101, which led to the integration of immigrants to Quebec into the francophone reality of the province—multiculturalism became an identifying feature of Quebec's society as well. The nouns *québécois* and *québécoise* have been largely transformed from ethnic into linguistic identifiers, and now are generally understood to refer to francophones of any ethnic origin who make that part of North America their home.

WHAT DOES MULTICULTURALISM OWE TO DUALISM?

The experience of living in a country with a profound ethnocultural division, I would argue, equipped Canadians with the capacity to accommodate the multiculturalism that is the product of postwar immigration. In fact, contained originally within one of the two founding communities, ironically enough, was cultural pluralism. Many of our Fathers of Confederation spoke with a Scottish accent. When Alexander Muir wrote his thumping anthem for British North America in 1867, it was "the thistle, shamrock, rose entwine, the maple leaf forever."

The fleur-de-lys was nowhere to be seen. Lest there be any doubt about what he had in mind, the last stanza begins:

> On merry England's far-famed land,
> May kind Heaven sweetly smile,
> God bless Old Scotland evermore,
> And Ireland's Emerald Isle!

Arising out of the coexistence of two quite different national communities, the British and the French, Canadians on each side of the divide learned to recognize their ignorance of the other. The sense of having a commanding or comprehensive knowledge of the land and its people is missing from the mental images of the nation that most citizens possess; understanding is inevitably partial and incomplete. Consider, by way of contrast, Randy Newman's song to America, "My Country," in which he sings of his people and says he knows 'em like the back of his own hand. When he sings this song, it works. It is somehow believable. An American can know, or can at least believe that he or she knows, the people of the United States in this way. America is an imagined community, and the bonds, for most Americans, are intimate at the level of the imagination. I always thought that the Canadianized version of "This land is your land, this land is my land; from Bonavista to Vancouver Island" was phony, in a way that, say, Gilles Vigneault's "Mon pays" absolutely is not. First of all, it is an American import. But more important, the song's sentiment implies the imagined intimacy of a cultural and national community, and *that* Canada has never been.

When I was a public servant in the Ontario government in the 1980s, I can well remember Robert Nixon, then the provincial treasurer, doing riffs in Cabinet about the apples and apple growers of southern Ontario, and about the main streets in the small towns of the province, and thinking that the man somehow *commanded* rural Ontario. He knew the look and smell and feel of the cities and towns and farms of the province, knew people everywhere and was known everywhere—except, I suspect, in metropolitan Toronto. I realized then that no national political leader could lay claim to that depth of understanding of Canada as a whole—not because of the limitations of our leaders, but because of the nature of the country itself. It did not then, and it does not today, lend itself to that level of comprehension. Indeed, neither do our large, immigrant-receiving metropolitan centres. They are warrens of diversity, with paths and trails running this way and that in patterns no one can fully fathom. The lineage of this sense of limited or partial understanding, which makes space for diversity, runs back to the earliest efforts at coexistence, back before Lord Durham to our beginnings, when the French and English, having struggled for imperial dominance, had to learn to live together somehow. For an immigrant, joining Canada has always been a more uncertain affair than is the case for his or her American counterpart. The preservation of migrant origin and identity has been more of an option north of the forty-ninth parallel than south.

The last four decades of national unity debate have engendered another characteristic of Canadian society, and it too has shaped the country's approach to multiculturalism. The Quebec sovereignty movement's sustained and powerful challenge to the very existence of the country has fostered an uneasy realization among many Canadians that their hold on Canada is a matter of contingent possession. It has not been possible during these years to assume that the country in which we live is effectively eternal, that it will always be there for us. We have had to recognize that it may not. The debate about the unity of the country has been almost entirely nonviolent, democratic and civil, and, with the assistance of the Supreme Court of Canada, we have learned that even the possible dismantling of one of the most successful countries in the world could be justified by the values we hold dear, and could be executed by democratic means. In its decision on the *Quebec Secession Reference*, the Supreme Court of Canada identified four fundamental, unstated principles that support Canada's constitutional order: federalism, democracy, constitutionalism and the rule of law, and respect for minority rights. It discovered a constitutional duty to negotiate with Quebec in the event that a clear majority of the citizens of Quebec in response to a clear question favoured the secession of the province. In doing so, it established in constitutional law the contingent nature of Canadian political affiliation.

Not for us the ringing declarations of France, *une république indivisible*, or Italy, *La Repubblica, una e indivisibile*, or Brazil, *formada pela união indissolúvel dos Estados e Municípios e do Distrito Federal*, or Australia, *one indissoluble Federal Commonwealth under the Crown of the United Kingdom of Great Britain and Ireland*: Canada, for its part, will exist as long as the Canadian people will it. As Ernest Renan says, a nation is a *plébiscite de tous les jours*. There are worse foundations on which to construct a political community. We are learning that the values for which the country stands can and should obtain even during its possible break-up. This lesson deprives our country of national glory, but it reminds us of the practical functions the state is expected to perform—in our country, to provide us with the blessings of peace, order and good government. It reminds us that the state itself is a human artefact, reared up to serve the interests and needs of the people for whom it is responsible, not an entity endowed with intrinsic moral or spiritual value. What we ask of immigrants is adherence to the constitution and the values underlying the constitutional order, not doctrinal acceptance of a universal patriotic creed. It is within the framework of these values, and especially our shared commitment to federalism and respect for minorities, that the accommodation of diversity that animates our multicultural policies and practices is to be found. Our national experience encourages the "desacralization" of the public realm. What Canadian today believes that it is the sacred duty of citizens to preserve the state and the national community, and that to seek the opposite is treason? We cannot afford that view. How, if we held that view, would we do business with the substantial minority of our population who hold democratically to the conviction that the Canadian experiment has more or less failed and should be wound up?

So the absence of a single, imagined national community, the awareness of the necessarily partial understanding of our country and its people, the consciousness of contingent possession, and the desacralization of the public realm—these realities, largely the product of our binational existence, have established the framework within which multiculturalism flourishes, both within Quebec and within the rest of Canada. They have fostered a prudential politics in this country, in which the task of the state is not the pursuit of an abstract theory of liberty or justice, but the search for practical accommodations that work. Muddling through is a vital if unacknowledged characteristic of our politics, leading our political leaders to get as far as they can in a day and to leave the rest for tomorrow. Muddling through, punctuated by moments of high drama is, I would say, how we have managed the national unity issue in this country, not pushing the envelope but responding to pressures as they arise, and seeking always the workable compromise. It is not glorious, but much that is glorious is not cut for human cloth; and it works, or at least it has worked up until now. The daily plebiscite has so far been favourable to Canada.

This strategy has largely formed the Canadian approach to the management of multiculturalism as well. The core of our success in this field lies not in a state plan or the application of a comprehensive rational design, but in a thousand accommodations in the schools and communities across the land.

COMMON CULTURE AND MULTIPLE CULTURES

Multiculturalism as a value emphasizes the mutually beneficial coexistence of different peoples within a single political community. The emphasis is typically placed on the existence of cultural diversity and the necessary framework that is required of the larger community if diversity is to be respected and to flourish. Until fairly recently, it was less frequently recognized that, if the framework itself is to be sustained, there must a common adherence, shared by all cultural groups, to certain fundamental values; in this sense "uniculturalism" must always underlie and sustain multiculturalism.[2] More than that, it must at certain points limit and constrain the expression of multiculturalism. In the midst of the furies unleashed in the aftermath of September 11, 2001, this has become a matter of acute international public concern, and, in fact, a matter of life and death. The politically motivated killings of Pim Fortuyn in May 2002 and Theo van Gogh in November 2004 in the Netherlands, a country traditionally immune from the political violence experienced elsewhere, have not only traumatized the Dutch but have also dramatized both the extent and the depth of the challenges that western societies face on the multicultural front. This issue is not, however, new. It was, after all, back in 1989 that the Ayatollah Khomeini pronounced a *fatwa* on Salman Rushdie for the publication of his *Satanic Verses* and called on the faithful to murder him, leading Rushdie to spend years of his life in protective custody.

The need to articulate and disseminate the common values upon which Canadian society rests has become more necessary as the diversity of Canadian society has deepened. With the elimination of racial bias from Canadian immigration policy in 1967, the pattern of immigration shifted dramatically. Prior to this policy change, something like 80 percent of Canadian immigration used to come from Europe or from countries of European heritage, such as the United States. In 2005, however, the US provided just over 3 percent of Canada's immigrants, and the United Kingdom and France, just over 2 percent each; today, there are fewer French immigrants than there are Iranian. The four top countries make up 41 percent of the total 2005 Canadian immigration of 262,236, and all of them are in Asia (China, India, the Philippines and Pakistan). The phenomenon of visible minorities has become much more significant; moreover, the cultural, racial, religious and linguistic distance between these new communities and the existing Canadian population is greater by far than was the distance between the resident Canadian population and the earlier migration of people, primarily from Europe and the United States. Today, less is shared among the communities at the outset, and much more ground has to be covered by both sides to close the gap between them. There is much greater scope for mutual suspicion, misunderstanding, and ethnic and racial tension. In addition, the fact that virtually all immigrants go to cities, rather than to the countryside as used to be the case a century ago, means that ethnocultural distance is combined with close geographical proximity, making the potential for friction that much greater.

The 1982 Canadian Charter of Rights and Freedoms has performed a critical role in regulating and supporting Canadian diversity. In this context, it does two things. It enunciates a system of rights to ensure the enjoyment of liberty for Canada's citizens and to provide legal remedy for those whose rights have been flouted. In a multicultural country, composed of two language communities, a formal system of rights enunciation and rights protection is an important device for ensuring maximum respect for freedom and equality of opportunity in a social environment of considerable diversity. In this sense, the Charter acknowledges differences, determines their relevance or irrelevance, and guarantees equitable treatment.

But the Charter does something else. In its enumeration of fundamental freedoms, its declaration of democratic, legal, equality and mobility rights, its provisions relating to official languages and minority language educational rights, its references to aboriginal rights and freedoms, to the multicultural heritage of Canadians, to the equal status of men and women, and to freedom of religion, the Canadian Charter formally expresses a number of fundamental values that stand as emblematic of Canadian society.

Thus the Canadian Charter of Rights and Freedoms recognizes multiculturalism and the diverse values of which it is composed, and at the same time places them in the context of a set of shared values, confirmed by law, that give structure and authority to the common culture underlying all Canadian life. The Charter, then, has been of immense assistance to Canadians in finding the means of accommodating the ethnocultural diversity of the Canadian community. Jurisprudence, grounded in its provisions, has significantly enlarged the place of aboriginal peoples in the Canadian social fabric. It has given constitutional standing to Canada's two official languages. The Charter has offered reassurance and support to immigrants from many lands, and a means of redress when their rights have been compromised. And it has done so by giving the courts and the Canadian people a legitimate vehicle for articulating what we share as Canadians. Among the things we share as Canadians is a widely held respect for diversity and a belief that—far from being a threat to Canadian society—this diversity is one of its great strengths and supports.

But in praising the Charter, let's not overdo it. First of all, it is not complete. It does not help our evolving understanding of Canadian citizenship or our increasingly sophisticated appreciation of multiculturalism to make the Charter carry more weight than it can bear. It is, after all, a document conceived and established at a particular historical moment, kept more or less current by evolving jurisprudence. Not all common Canadian values are included within it. It would be the rare Canadian who does not believe in private property, for example; yet that as a right did not make the cut in 1982. Equally, the protection of sexual orientation was not included, but in recent case law the Supreme Court has held that sexual orientation constitutes a prohibited ground of discrimination under the equality provisions of the Charter. This latter, surely, is an example of Canadian society evolving over the years and coming gradually to accept as a principle of justice something that was not generally recognized as such in 1982. And, as often as not, the courts follow public opinion, rather than lead it.

Second, there is such a thing as bad law. Lawyers and philosophers have wrestled with this phenomenon, where the law is not just an ass, but positively noxious in its foundation and effects. One need not look only to a place like Nazi Germany to find examples of bad law; there are ample examples that can be found in our past: for example, laws relating to the involuntary sterilization of mental incompetents, the imposition of the Chinese head tax, the internment of the Japanese during World War II, not to mention the historical exclusion of women and the propertyless from the political process. Lest the argument is made that these affronts to civilized life are all pre-Charter and therefore could not happen today, bear in mind that the Americans interned their Japanese community during World War II as well, and they had a constitutional Bill of Rights at the time. Flagrant discrimination against black Americans existed for years right alongside that same US Bill of Rights. Unless we are so arrogant as to believe that it is only our ancestors who are capable of making such egregious mistakes, it would be prudent to entertain the possibility that we and our descendants are and will be equally capable of committing what, with the passing of time, will be regarded as terrible errors in the manner in which we treat our fellow citizens, and that these errors could well be reflected in law.

Third, there is the question of the sweep or reach of the Charter. Is the Charter so unanswerably perfect that there need be no hesitation with the idea of extending its grasp over the whole of society? Lawyers speak of the dialectical relationship among the constitution, the legislature and the courts; many welcome what they see as the positive friction that exists among these three institutions, arguing that it is at the interstices of policy and practice where social progress can best be made. Equally, the friction that exists between a country's legal norms and its community beliefs and practices can foster a fruitful exchange by which a society moves forward as a fuller understanding of the requirements of justice make themselves manifest. That calls for debate, but it does not argue for extending the sweep of the Charter into every nook and cranny of our lives. Indeed, to do so would be to remove the creative friction and to staunch the very conversation from which a liberal society benefits.

The Charter is an instrument of liberal constitutionalism. Liberalism is grounded not only in a recognition of and respect for the individual human person, but also in the recognition of the distinction between the public and the private. When, in 1967, Pierre Trudeau as minister of justice said that there is no place for the state in the bedrooms of the nation, he was voicing his conviction that the role of the state was and had to be limited. It was not the state's job to regulate consensual, private relations among adults. Today, that principle of restraint seems to have been widely accepted insofar as it relates to matters of sexual practice and personal or lifestyle choices. No one — and certainly not the government — has a right to tell me how to lead my life, so long as I am not harming any one and so long as I am not imposing my life choices on others.

That restraint is often less in evidence in the manner in which western countries accommodate cultural pluralism. France sees nothing contradictory between its commitment to democratic republicanism and its March 2004 ban on students wearing conspicuous religious garb or symbols in its public schools.[3] Indeed, forbidding Muslim headscarves, Sikh turbans, Jewish skull caps and large Christian crosses is regarded by many as being perfectly consistent with a commitment to secular liberalism, and one of the ways in which that form of liberalism is protected. The uncompromising secularity of French public institutions is meant to create a space of freedom and equality for all of France's citizens, no matter what their private religious beliefs may be. In Britain, Jack Straw, the Labour leader of the House of Commons, mused in October 2006 about the discomfort caused to members of the majority community by women in a minority community wearing what they choose — in this case, Muslim women wearing the niqab or veil.[4] In Canada, we have had debates of this kind as well. Recall the controversy a decade and a half ago over the right of uniformed Sikh RCMP officers to wear their turbans, and the more recent question of whether Sikh students should be allowed to carry their *kirpan* or ceremonial daggers into the classroom.[5]

There are two things worth noting about these cases. First of all, with the possible exception of the last case, which raises reasonable concerns about school safety, the issues of concern do not involve matters of conduct but rather what one might call manifestations of identity: the burka, chador and niqab; the turban, the cross, the kippah and the Star of David. As such, they speak to questions of belief, not questions of behaviour. On what liberal grounds can these presentations of self or assertions of community membership justifiably attract censure or restraint? It seems to me that in the absence of plausible links to unacceptable conduct, there are no grounds for restraint.

The second thing worth noting is that it is only some manifestations of identity that occasion contemporary anxiety or concern. We do not bother ourselves with Native headdresses or Indian necklaces. We accept the sweet grass ceremony, even when the ritual interposes itself in the normal processes of western-style meetings and conferences. These are seen as celebrations of aboriginal identity, and—aware of the injustices of the past—we belatedly celebrate the images that remind us that an aboriginal reality still exists in this country. We welcome aboriginal efforts to preserve Native tongues, even though we sought to suppress them in years gone by. The kippah or yarmulke, the ringlets and dangling strings of orthodox Jews are curiosities, nothing more. But it is the manifestations of Muslim identity that people in western countries find deeply troubling today, and for an obvious reason. The terrorism that threatens western cities and institutions is associated in the public mind with Islam. Many of the suicide bombers and terrorists have explained their actions by reference to the struggle of the Muslim faithful against the West. Westerners have learned, not to understand the Muslim world, but to fear it, so physical manifestations of that world occasion unease.

NEGOTIATING THE INTERFACE BETWEEN PRIVATE AND PUBLIC

For liberals, the frame of reference and the primary unit of analysis is the individual; the classic dilemma has to do with the establishment of the proper relationship between the state and the individual citizen. But the assumptions of liberal individualism are not so helpful when what is at issue are the entitlements and prerogatives that groups and members of groups should be understood to possess in a free and democratic society, and it is here that the challenges of multiculturalism typically arise.

To think our way through this issue, it is useful to reflect briefly on the views of people who might be called philosophical conservatives, because the conception of society of people who share this broad outlook is somewhat different from that of liberal individualists. Conservatives see a profound and intimate relationship between the human individual and the groups of which he or she is a part. Human beings from birth are embedded in a complex web of associations and practices; their identity is formed as a result of the dialectical relationship they have with the communities in which they are embedded. These associations and practices are not adequately understood as the product of the state or as the rational constructions of autonomous individuals; there is an important sense in which they precede and make possible the individual and rest on a footing more fundamental even than that of the state. The regulation and control of the political community owe as much to this web of private institutions and customary practices as they do to the authority of the state and the actions of government. Understanding the significance of this private realm of civil society, totalitarian regimes typically do their best to destroy it, leaving the individual naked and alone before the power of the state, bereft of the supports of family, neighbourhood, tribe, religious institutions and voluntary organizations, creating a grotesque perversion of the assumptions of individualism, where the individualism of autonomous and responsible citizens is replaced by the rootless anomie of subjects and victims, who become little more than units of obedience.

While the dominant discourse in western democracies is that of liberal individualism, the lived reality is more complex and draws on other forms of political and social understanding, including the thinking that underlies what I am calling conservatism. The presuppositions of conservatism are helpful in our effort to think through some of the issues currently related to multiculturalism, for one of the beliefs of this style of political thinking is that it is good, both for society and for the state, to have structures of authority and action—institutions and practices—that are independent of the state—families, local authorities, religious institutions, commercial organizations, voluntary associations and the like. These can act as a brake and control on the political power of the state; they can offer human-scale contexts in which citizens engage in social and community life; they make more likely the diversity and experimentation that contributes to social advancement; they contribute to the density and richness of civil society.

These are, I think, much the kind of justifications offered in support of multiculturalism. Why do we celebrate multiculturalism? Why was its preservation and enhancement introduced as a value into the 1982 Charter of Rights and Freedoms? Why do Canadians generally regard it as a good thing? Presumably, part of the reason is because there is a simple social reality that one cannot ignore. Canada is a country of immigrants from many different lands and cultures; this is a fact. But multiculturalism enjoys a higher status than is justified by its existence as a simple sociological reality.

If the intent is to preserve and enhance cultural pluralism in Canada, this means, at a minimum, that ethnic, religious and linguistic differentiation of some kind is seen as a positive benefit. The question is what kind of differentiation? If multiculturalism is meant to be understood as a structural feature of Canadian society, it must presumably relate to more than folklore, dance and ethnic publications. It needs to receive expression in relation to things that matter. It needs to have some impact on the power relations in Canadian society, and ultimately on the cultural character and practices of the country as a whole. Has that happened? I would say that to a noticeable extent, it has, and one of the ways it has been allowed to happen is by the state exercising restraint in the reach of its regulatory activity. Many private institutions and practices fall outside the range of the Charter of Rights and Freedoms, and in some cases their norms diverge from the provisions of the Charter. Several examples of this sort—for example, gender inequality in certain religious institutions—are discussed in this volume. This means that members of religious and other institutions are entitled to engage in certain practices that are repugnant to the majority of their fellow citizens.

What should the state do about it? In many cases, it should do nothing. In other cases, the preservation and protection of the "uniculture" underlying multiculturalism, not to mention the protection of the persons entitled to its benefits, oblige intervention. Let us admit straight off that sorting out what falls into which category is a difficult and fraught challenge. It seems to me that religious rituals that deny women an equal role fall into the "do nothing" category, as does the choice of some churches not to perform same-sex marriages, so long as the religious adherents have the option to exit and to associate themselves with alternative religious institutions and persons seeking same-sex marriages have a civil-law option (and, in all likelihood, the prospect of a better welcome at other churches). Should the state indirectly support such organizations by giving them charitable status and tax breaks? Ultimately, probably not; but it is not inappropriate for the state to give some weight in its policy making to a community's historical experience and to the institutions that are the product of that history. Societies, after all, evolve over time, not in rationally required leaps and bounds. The genital mutilation of young girls, however, falls clearly into the "intervention" category. The claims of cultural diversity cannot trump the prohibition of a practice that is clearly inconsistent with the respect for persons required in a free and democratic society.

But many cases do not fall definitively into one category or the other. Here some circumspection is no bad thing, as is the granting of time to a society to help it adjust to newly emerging realities and pressures. The traditional societies of English and French Canada have been leavened and enriched by their encounters with multiculturalism. All parties to the exchange have been altered by it and, in the process, Canada itself has been transformed.

Communities live in space and time. They occupy a physical space—a territory—but they also live in and through time. Given the relentless "present mindedness" of the contemporary world, too little attention is paid to the temporal dimension within which societies and individuals exist. A society, after all, can be understood as an unending series of human transactions, affirming and reaffirming a will to perpetuate a common existence. The act of living together, one day after another, solving problems, making things work, is after all how most free societies hang together. And time, well used, is a powerful negotiator. With time we adapt, we enlarge our views, we accommodate ourselves to new situations: with time we domesticate what initially seemed to be alien and troublesome forces; with time we change; with time we make friends.

Canada, by and large, has made time an ally in its accommodation of cultural pluralism. It has used the time it has been given, not to deny change or to arrest the processes of history, but to allow the forces of social and cultural transformation to work their way into all corners of Canadian life. Multiculturalism points to a set of human encounters in which everyone is changed and from which everyone benefits. In the unfolding story of Canadian multiculturalism, the Charter of Rights and Freedoms, while of critical importance, is more of a policy taker than a policy maker; it is Canadian society itself, especially metropolitan Canada, that is breaking new ground in response to one of the 21st century's most critical challenges.

NOTES

1 In the preparation of this chapter, I have drawn from the Morton Lecture, which I gave at Trent University some time ago. It appeared in the *Journal of Canadian Studies* under the title of "Lord Durham Then and Now" (vol. 25, no. 1 [Spring 1990], pp. 5–23).

2 Equally, shared fundamental values must underlie biculturalism, too, but—particularly since Quebec's Quiet Revolution of the early 1960s—differences in fundamental values and convictions have not really been at the core of Canada's national unity tensions. The philosophy of Quebec's *Charte québécoise des droits et libertés de la personne*, for example, is much like that of Canada's Charter of Rights and Freedoms.

3 *Loi no. 2004–228 du 15 mars 2004 encadrant, en application du principe de laïcité, le port de signes ou de tenues manifestant une appartenance religieuse dans les écoles, collèges et lycées publics.*

4 The Straw controversy had been preceded by the case of the dismissal of a British-born Muslim teaching assistant from Headfield Church of England Junior School for wearing the veil in classes.

5 In 1990, the government of Canada lifted its ban against turbaned RCMP officers. On March 2, 2006, the Supreme Court of Canada unanimously overturned a Quebec school board's ban on carrying *kirpan* at school, ruling that it infringed students' religious freedom under the Canadian Charter of Rights and Freedoms.

REFERENCES

Acton, John Emerich Edward Dalberg, Baron. 1964. "Nationality." In *Essays on Freedom and Power*, ed. Gertrude Himmelfarb, pp. 166–195. Cleveland: World Publishing.

Durham, John George Lambton, Earl of. 1982. *Lord Durham's Report: An Abridgement of the Report on the Affairs of British North America by Lord Durham*, ed. Gerald M. Craig. Ottawa: Carleton University Press.

Mill, John Stuart. 1958. *Considerations on Representative Government*, ed. Currin V. Shields. Indianapolis: Bobbs-Merrill.

Canada—J'accuse/J'adore: Extracts from a Memoir

John Meisel

At a conference at the Munk Centre for International Studies in Toronto not long ago, I bumped into my friend Janice Gross Stein, its chatelaine. As always, I was delighted to see her, but there was a particular frisson this time because it gave me the opportunity to tell her how greatly I enjoyed and admired an article she had recently published in the *Literary Review of Canada* on some of her reflections on, and experiences in, multicultural Canada. I was, it seems, one of a great many fans: the piece elicited so much interest (and controversy) that an enlarged version was being morphed into the lead chapter in a book exploring her principal ideas: this book, in fact.

I allowed that, in the ongoing process of trying to write my memoirs, I had drafted a slightly naughty but deadly serious chapter on Canada, which touches on a number of related themes. Generous to a fault, as ever, she agreed to read it and then concluded that parts would fit nicely between the covers of this volume. I was hijacked, or perhaps I just cunningly hitched a ride. So here we are.

This volume explores the many faces of multiculturalism in Canada and how they relate to other features of our society. My own story started as a straightforward set of reflections on the country, without necessarily privileging a discussion of our demographic heterogeneity. Unwittingly and significantly, however, it often drifted onto this terrain, indicating that it is hard for some of us, perhaps all of us, to ignore this pivotal feature of the land. Nor are these questions about culture and identity simple or unidirectional. Ambivalence and complexity permeate the whole ball of wax.

When developing my original ideas, I was struck by how many of our national failings actually grow out of, or are related to, our strengths. Janus came to mind. He, you remember, is the Roman god usually represented with two faces, one looking forward and the other backward. He can, therefore, assume two sometimes opposing miens. This essay's heading, indicating that Canada both pleases and worries me, reflects the Janus-like nature of our national character. In determining which end of the scale wins, I find myself coming down unequivocally on one side.

Nevertheless I am constantly compelled to qualify, modify and reassess my reading of events because they simultaneously possess positive and negative features. Goals pursued for a particular set of reasons are challenged when other imperatives enter the equation. In the language of this volume, some of the features of multiculturalism clash with certain provisions of the Canadian Charter of Rights and Freedoms; understanding and tolerance can turn into lack of principle; practices such as sexism in the synagogue, female circumcision or beating one's wife fundamentally violate prevailing values; generosity toward immigrants or refugees may in some instances threaten national interest; individual freedom can endanger the common good; preserving the folkways of newcomers sometimes interferes with age-old traditions and vice versa; objections to the public observance of Christmas or Chanukah are seen by some as an onslaught on habits hallowed by time. This overly long list of examples touches on only a tiny fraction of the contrarieties caused by the diversity of Canada's population.

Despite the many problems arising from such complex and often opposing factors, the lavish presence of so many diverse cultures immeasurably enriches the Canadian experience. But, of course, it also generates a vast profusion of personal and public issues needing resolution. That these coexist with an equally daunting number of conundrums unrelated or only remotely connected to ethnicity reduces their salience and the attention they receive. Possibly this is as it should be. I return to that question at the end of this excerpt from my memoir, which begins here.

NAMBY-PAMBY NATIONALISM

The Canada that greeted the Meisels in 1942, and particularly our province of Ontario, bore numerous hallmarks of a British land. An intense involvement in the war, ranging from widespread voluntary enrolment for service overseas to vigorous efforts by patriotic ladies knitting socks for inclusion in parcels to the troops and for civilians in the Blitz, ubiquitous reminders of the royal connection such as playing "God Save the King (Queen)" before the commencement of the main feature in the cinema or families listening together to the broadcast of the monarch's speech on Christmas Day, crests and plaques on buildings, and the nature and language of most political institutions—these were only some of the highly visible reminders of the British connection. A great many people one met were transplanted Brits. Since then, and particularly since the end of the Second World War, these and other vestiges of the link with Albion have been gradually obliterated. War brides stopped arriving, and the postwar influx of British immigrants turned into a trickle and dried up. Canada drifted from the British into the US orbit and became ever more inexorably Americanized. Eventually, with the adoption in 1982 of the Charter of Rights and Freedoms, even one of the cardinal principles of the British political system—parliamentary supremacy—fell by the wayside.

But important vestiges of British political culture have survived. They include, among other things, the commitment to the rule of law, a truly independent judiciary, a comparatively very high level of public morality, minimal corruption, insistence on a generally competent, non-partisan public service and, exceptions notwithstanding, pervasive civility. For those whose memory goes back far enough, or who dabble in Canadian history, the legacy of the British "mother country" is self-evident.

Another contributor to the Canadian collective psyche is much less obvious and even denied by some. It arises out of the presence of what is variously described as the Lower Canadian, Quebec or French fact. One aspect is particularly germane to the present part of my story. It is that the history and numeric weight of Canadians of British and French origin are respectively so hefty that members of each cannot escape being aware of the presence of the other. This recognition is re-inforced by the impact Canada's duality has had on politics and pub-lic life. It has also been strengthened by important policies, such as the Official Languages Act, and by major public inquiries, of which the Royal Commission on Bilingualism and Biculturalism was the most prominent and far-reaching.

Whether consciously or unconsciously, willingly or reluctantly, vir-tually all Canadians become aware of the presence of the other group and of the need for the country to accommodate it. A great many Cana-dians have, therefore, an incentive for tolerating, or at least coexisting with, another partner. This incentive has, for demographic reasons, been most evident in central and eastern Canada, but a similar spur exists elsewhere. In the Prairies and British Columbia, for instance, the major "other" ethnic group was rarely French, but usually another of the many immigrant clusters making up the Canadian mosaic. But here, too, the presence of diverse nationalities compelled the evolution of outlooks, practices and policies permitting a reasonable coexistence of individuals coming from varied backgrounds.

By and large Canada has avoided both the melting-pot mentality and the segregationist zeal evident in many other jurisdictions. Thus the dualism growing out of the country's early history, while still play-ing an important role, has gradually been joined by multicultural poli-cies designed to facilitate the self-fulfillment of individuals and groups from a wide range of origins. The arrival of so-called "visible minori-ties" has created further complexities challenging the art of coexis-tence. We are still learning how to adjust, but can derive some satisfac-tion from the fact that, compared to a great many other places, Canada has not made too bad a fist of coping with the migration patterns of the twenty-first century. Indeed, our handling of a bustling ethnic hetero-geneity, though far from perfect, is something of a model for other countries and facilitates our fitting well into the newly emerging global society. Still, as we shall see, there are also liabilities.

Canada's British and French core fused with other elements. This and the somewhat polyglot character of our ethnic and cultural mix have contributed to the emergence of a benign, open and humane political culture. Compared to a great many so-called civilized countries, Canada has attained a praiseworthy level of enlightenment. Think of issues such as capital punishment, gun control, equality between the sexes, same-sex marriage and variations in sexual preference, or the rights of immigrants and refugees. All this adds up to Canada enjoying uncommonly high standards of civility and even propriety in day-to-day private and public life. No wonder international surveys invariably rank Canada among the very best of places in which to live or conduct business.

Although exceptions inevitably occur, Canadians tend to eschew brash aggressiveness and value politeness. *Spy*, a now defunct New York satirical monthly run by a Canadian, twenty years ago carried a story about Canada, when this country played a prominent role in American entertainment, real estate, retailing and other fields. To protect the United States from being overrun, it argued tongue-in-cheek, Yanks had to learn how to tell Canadians from Americans. An appended "Canadian-spotters Field Manual" provided many hints, including that Canadians never forget to say "please" and "thank you," even to the bank machine. It also noted that, in a job interview, the Canadian will ask about the pension plan before inquiring about the starting salary.

Unlike most other countries, Canada has lacked a clearly defined and strong sense of self. One of our most characteristic and perhaps defining national traits is, in fact, a constant preoccupation with—and uncertainty about—what sort of country we are, other than *not* being American. While this can be tedious, it also has some attractive features. Our search for the Canadian essence leads us constantly to examine not only the national status quo but also to ask ourselves to what we should aspire as a collectivity. There is no smug pride but a search for desirable goals. Regional variations exist in all this and it is important to note that Quebeckers are much more Quebec- than Canada-centred. They know exactly what and who they are and tend to be much less concerned about the rest of the country. But many of the country's characteristics and decisions willy-nilly affect Quebec and even more the francophone minorities in New Brunswick, Ontario and elsewhere.

As one who has had the misfortune of being uncomfortably close to the baleful byproducts of breast-beating nationalism in central Europe, I greatly appreciate Canada's somewhat namby-pamby approach to *la patrie*—a term, by the way, for which there is a literal English translation (fatherland) but one missing the rich patriotic nuance of the French. Léon Dion tellingly distinguished, in one of his autobiographical reflections, between Canada as his *pays* (country) and Quebec as his *patrie*. This difference has, in reverse form, more recently been invoked by Michael Ignatieff. But, as we shall see, the absence of a boastful nationalism also exacts a price.

Another striking Canadian characteristic, leading me to the "*j'adore*" as opposed to the "*j'accuse*" pole in my title, concerns a significant difference with the United States. When our proximity to and affinity with the US are recalled, Canada is surprisingly more accepting of "collective" goals as distinct from "individualistic" ones. This sentiment wanes and waxes over time and is currently under stress, but there is an enduring commitment in Canada to the public interest. While not immune to the rampant individualism exuded by modern capitalism and particularly the US, Canadians nevertheless readily welcome state intervention if it conveys some shared benefit.

Among the themes of our interminable soul-searching about the nature of Canadian identity one commonly proposed theory even argues that it is our commitment to universal medical insurance and the social safety net that defines us and binds us together. There are indeed numerous instances of a Canadian attachment to some community-centred good as distinct from an individualistic one. The welfare state has done much better here than to the south of us. Equalization payments are accepted as normal, enabling the federal government to channel funds from the richer sections of the country to the poorer, and mildly social democratic or otherwise progressive parties such as the Co-operative Commonwealth Federation, the New Democratic Party and the Parti Québécois attract substantial proportions of electoral support. They have formed governments in some provinces, and their presence federally has not only affected the orientation of other parties, particularly the Liberals, but, in periods of minority Liberal governments, they have also had significant impact on the direction of public policy. Likewise, in contradistinction to Washington, lobbies for particular industries, regions or ideologies wield considerably less power, although the bargaining clout of Quebec comes close.

A lot of the foregoing, as I have warned, presents only a part of the picture, but it does convey much of the essential flavour. And whatever the grim facts, this is what a great many Canadians dabbling in these matters believe, and what they want their country to be like. When judging people, it is important to consider not only what they *do* but also that to which they *aspire*. One of Canadians' most attractive and endearing features is that their self-image and national ideal so closely correspond to the benign, appealing, kind, tolerant, slightly milquetoastian model I have just sketched.

TARNISHING THE NICE-GUY IMAGE

What about the other side? Is there, to use the memorable line from Stella Gibbons's *Cold Comfort Farm*, something nasty in the woodshed? There is, and oddly enough, as I observed above, some of the causes are related to or even grow out of a few of the characteristics recited above, which seemingly make Canadians such paragons. Certain of the country's shortcomings are mere irritations but others are serious and truly troubling.

I mentioned, approvingly, the Canadians' less than fanatical attachment to their country. But that the relationship is often lukewarm also entails costs. I regularly ski and hike in Austria. Some of my gripes about my Canadian homeland are informed by that experience. Most goods in the stores in the Alpine republic, unlike in Canada, are domestically made and prominently display a stylized red and white "A," the logo identifying their origin. Furthermore, Austrian enterprises have for the most part not been allowed to fall into foreign hands. Compare this with Canada, where so many of our industrial and other economic icons have been, and continue to be, acquired by non-resident owners unmindful of and unconcerned with the broader Canadian context. Domestically owned Austrian firms are different; they cater to the needs of local employees and communities. This is one of the reasons why the unemployment rate in Austria has consistently been lower than in Canada, although the gap has narrowed since Austria has joined the European Union. Equally important, the proportional investment in science and technology by Austrian industry far exceeds ours.

A less significant, but tell-tale and to me fiercely grating difference between the two countries concerns the use of national emblems. "Our" village in the Tirol—a skiing and hiking paradise—is seasonally overrun by German and, when the ubiquitous mushrooms mushroom, Italian tourists. But you'd never know it from its appearance, only from the accents and licence plates. Unlike in Southern Ontario, where my ire over this issue is constantly fanned, you never see a foreign flag. But there are lots of reminders of where you are. Every hut or chalet offering meals (and what meals!) flies a large red and white Austrian flag or the Tirolian emblem. Austrians love and are proud of their country. To flaunt a foreign flag for the sake of making a few shekels would seem *lese-majesté* and quite inappropriate. The servile, grovelling Canadian way of trying to attract American customers by mounting their flag strikes me as self-abasement. At the same time it misses an opportunity to convey to our American visitors that we prize our country and identity, that we *are* different and separate, and that we are glad to welcome them to the Canadian way. Promiscuous willingness to display foreign emblems bespeaks a relatively low and superficial attachment to one's own. I refuse to set foot in an establishment displaying the US flag except in a dire emergency.

Another of the likeable attributes imputed to Canadians, as I noted, is their tendency to be laidback, polite and inclined to avoid controversy. Nice. But can these qualities be carried too far? Various factors cause people either to espouse or avoid an issue. Being passive is only one of them but it affects other, more substantive motives. Canadians have been uncaring or inhuman, sometimes scandalously so, with respect to the plight of certain minorities.

In the mid-nineteenth century Chinese labour was good enough to be assigned a critical part in the construction of a transcontinental

Canadian railway, a major nation-building feat if ever there was one. Their reward was a costly and humiliating head tax imposed on every Chinese person entering Canada once the railroad was finished. And Chinese immigration was prohibited outright in 1923. The ban was not repealed until 1947. Quite recently, the Canadian government apologized for the treatment accorded the Chinese immigrants long ago, thereby acknowledging errors of the past.

Ex post facto compensation for former wrongs are sometimes resorted to by guilt-ridden governments, and often demanded by aggrieved ethnic groups or, more often, by their descendants. Even well-intentioned steps by ashamed authorities raise some tough questions, however. On what basis are descendants, who may never have suffered, to be compensated? What are the grounds for offering relief to those who have been injured and what constitutes a reasonable restitution? How far back in time should one go? If some communities are compensated, why not others? Are there clear indications which past transgressions call for redress, and which do not? How do we avoid catering to well-organized, politicized causes while neglecting equally deserving ones without champions? Can one resist being exploited by individuals, law firms, groups, organizations and even political parties opportunistically exploiting embarrassing historical situations?

The 1939 refusal by the Mackenzie King government to allow a ship carrying 900 Jewish refugees from the Nazis to land in Canada, aping the rejection of numerous other countries, is another example of gross intolerance, making Canada an unconscious and indirect accomplice to the Holocaust. Fred Blair, Canada's top immigration official, when asked how many Jewish refugees Canada would accept, flippantly replied "None is too many"—a response that provided Irving Abella and Harold Troper with the title of their classic book on anti-Semitism in Canada. The ship with its human cargo had to return to Germany, where most of the passengers were eventually exterminated. The incident is unbelievable and horrible, a reminder that Canada's behaviour with respect to human rights is far from blameless.

There are other signs of recurring racial prejudice and intolerance of minorities threatening to the country's nice-guy image sketched above. Indefensible behaviour toward the Chinese is now ancient history and perhaps invites us to blame it on something other than a national failing, perhaps merely on the collective callousness of youth. Canada was a colony then and a very young polity. But the racist policies of Mackenzie King and Frederick Blair, his immigration sidekick, are almost within living memory. And there is a pressing and very contemporary issue in this country that betrays unmistakably racist overtones.

The treatment accorded Canada's aboriginal population not only casts a deep shadow on past policies and decisions, but also continues to confront us with a monumental moral and policy challenge. There is little evidence so far that we really have the will to recognize and respond to it. Most members of the political class are too complacent, too comfortable with the status quo to see and respond to the magnitude of the crisis afflicting a large number of Indians, Métis, Inuit and Innu. Conditions rooted in their early relationships with European settlers and conquerors can only be addressed adequately by an unprecedented national effort.

The facts are appalling. Every social indicator, whether related to health, infant and adult mortality, education, residence, physical and mental well-being, crime rates, legal status, or economic and psychic satisfaction offers proof that, compared to other groups, the aboriginal population, taken as a whole, whether residing on a reservation, in a city core or on Arctic ice, lags far behind, and not just by a whisker but by thousands of leagues. Over the years, remedial measures were tried, and they still are at an accelerating and intensifying rate, but the results are negligible. In fairness, it must be acknowledged that the problems are unimaginably intractable and the cast of characters involved is extremely complex and possessed of inevitable human failings. My disappointment is less with the paucity of results than with the fact that Canadians and their leaders have never shaken off the "business as usual" mode. Truly heroic approaches are needed, but the sense of urgency required is stifled by our complacent acceptance of the myth that, all in all, we are doing all right.

CANADIANS IN CHARTERLAND

Lack of success in making sufficient headway on the aboriginal front contrasts vividly with other areas marked by truly revolutionary changes. Strangely, the closely related field of human rights has, as I noted, been fundamentally redefined with far-reaching consequences for individual behaviour and group rights. One of the results of the constitutional reforms orchestrated by Pierre Elliott Trudeau in the early 1980s was to patriate the Constitution as well as to define numerous basic rights for Canadians and enshrine them in the Charter of Rights and Freedoms. While this has done little specifically for the aboriginal population, it has had an extended impact on the power of politicians by subjecting laws passed by legislatures to extensive judicial review. Laws, much more than before, express what the courts say they do and hence we are governed not only by Parliament but also by judges.

"Charterland," as some observers call our new constitutional ambience and the general atmosphere it has engendered, enlarged the rights of some groups and has accordingly enhanced their self-esteem and opportunities. Previously constrained collectivities have, in the currently favoured jargon, become empowered and are offered fuller citizenship. Women are one example, as are some ethnic minorities and gays. This calls for applause; it has made us a fairer, better and stronger country. But it is short-sighted and self-deceiving to ignore that in addition to benefits there are also liabilities, particularly because of the excessive zeal that is usually displayed, and perhaps needed, when past errors or shortcomings are being redressed. Affirmative action often perpetrates unfairness and reverse discrimination. The crotchety part of me is troubled by several such developments.

Among them is a tendency to obliterate or diminish values and symbols associated with traditional, long-established communities. One example is the fear of some well-meaning people that the display at Christmas time in public places or company premises of crêches or other reminders of the Nativity might offend or otherwise harm non-Christians. This is bothersome on at least two counts: Christianity is a central and powerful component of Canada's history and heritage. Although attitudes to it have changed, it is an integral part of the country's tradition that enriches all groups living here. Many of the attractive features (as well as some less appealing ones) of Canadian culture have their roots in Christian churches and sects. To diminish or hide Canada's Christian heritage is a form of amputation and suppression of the past.

Second, irrespective of its spiritual content, Christmas has become a much-loved social and family ceremony and occasion. True, commercial interests have appropriated it and robbed it of much spiritual meaning. Nevertheless, despite its having become, in some circles, a grotesque and obscene display of conspicuous consumption, it binds large numbers of Canadians together, and not only Christians. To banish it from public sight because its visible celebration might offend other faiths is to short-change important traditional components of society and to pamper overly sensitive minorities. It is, in fact, an example of one of our dubious national traits.

Attempts to blot out long-established cultural patterns for the sake of sparing the feelings of minorities are a relatively new phenomenon in Canada. They reflect fundamental differences in ideas about the rights and privileges of old settlers or their descendants on the one hand and newcomers on the other. In the early 1940s, when my family and I came here, we were hell-bent on fitting in. An important means was to respect and honour the prevailing ways of doing things. The idea that these ought to be altered to suit our preferences was unthinkable and ludicrous. Accordingly, in all the places we had lived we immediately started to learn the local language, if we did not already know it. We did this even if it was not a "major" one, as was the case during our brief sojourn in Holland. I blush to admit that we were not bold enough to tackle Arabic when in Casablanca. Respect for the prevailing customs went so far as to make us speak Czech in an exceedingly low voice when in public, so as not to grate on local ears. And, although privately continuing to celebrate our own traditions (e.g., Christmas dinner on the evening of December 24th), we fell in with such innovations as tricks and treats on Halloween and turkey on Thanksgiving, joys then unknown in central Europe.

These relatively superficial things had their roots in the assumption that now that we were in Canada, we ought to behave like Canadians. Although we never articulated this, even to ourselves, our behaviour likely arose out of the belief that in the normal course of events, countries and their cultures reflect some communal values. These deserved respect and normally took precedence over individual preferences, even when these were shared by some of their constituent groups. The dictum "When in Rome, do as the Romans do" meant something to us and was applied.

I am not sure whether the stance we adopted, often quite unconsciously, reflected our origins in a small country in central Europe, our status as quasi-refugees, our personal family history or just the times. What I am sure of is that it must strike present-day Canadians as hopelessly anachronistic. Most new settlers, particularly if they share a profound religious belief, feel entitled to exactly the same "space" they enjoyed at home, even if it clashes with Canadian norms. At the root of this difference is the conviction, in one case, that the communal values of a country exact recognition and obeisance and, in another, that ethnic and religious traditions take precedence. In some ways, this is just a partly secular variant of the age-old conundrum about the appropriate relationship between church and state. There is a tendency in Canada these days to resolve it in a one-sided manner, favouring the new and discriminating against the old. While this provides a welcoming climate for arriving outsiders, it may alienate long-established citizens and undermine the world to which they have become accustomed and which they love. It may also, on occasion, lead to the importation of practices and forms of behaviour incompatible with prevailing values and conventions.

Canadians bask in the knowledge that they enjoy an enviable reputation for generally holding progressive and humane positions on many social issues. But here, too, they have a propensity to overdo it. As in the example I just noted, we all too easily lean over backward, sometimes making fools of ourselves. An area in which this has become something of a joke, albeit one masking serious consequences, relates to the application of the Charter. Its architects have assured Canadians that the extensive human rights and privileges it guarantees apply to anyone *on Canadian territory*. There are innumerable instances of illegal immigrants or refugees, some with highly questionable backgrounds, playing the Canadian legal system and the free services it provides for all they are worth. Appeal follows appeal, loophole suc-ceeds loophole, enabling opportunists to exploit and live off Cana-dian taxpayers for ten years or more before being deported. The legal costs are astronomical. This sort of thing makes us international laugh-ingstocks and attracts more suspect arrivals.

In a related sphere, Canadian citizenship and passports seem to be available to a great many people who have no intention of joining Canadian society and life. Before Hong Kong severed its ties with Britain to become an integral part of China, many wealthy Hong Kongers managed to become Canadian citizens merely to acquire an insurance policy in case things eventually went badly wrong. Canada was not seen as a treasured homeland but as a convenient site for a sort of Rent-a-Passport transaction.

Likewise, during the Hezbollah–Israeli conflict in 2006, the world was startled by the huge number of Canadian citizens trapped by the fighting. Some were Canadians of Lebanese origin holidaying in their former homeland. But a great many had acquired a Canadian passport and subsequently returned to live in the country they really called their home.

Issues of citizenship and passports are immensely complex, diffi-cult to define and to regulate. I have the impression that Canada is less successful than some other countries in preventing the illegal ac-quisition of its passports. A man of uncertain origin recently accused of being a Russian spy, court records revealed, managed to obtain three Canadian passports in the space of seven years. Is this, too, a manifestation of our easygoing style and of the generally tepid na-ture of Canadianism?

Another noteworthy area where Canadian practices and conven-tions go to ridiculously tolerant lengths is the treatment by the media of crimes committed by members of certain minorities. Political cor-rectness or some other fussy shibboleth prevents the relevant reports from revealing the ethnic or religious origin of the people involved. Au-thorities and the media here sometimes collude to withhold informa-tion. When, in 2006, the police arrested 18 people for allegedly engag-ing in terrorist plots, the RCMP said that they represented broad strata of Canadian society and *The Toronto Star* asserted that it was difficult to find a common denominator among them. In fact, they were all Muslims and many attended the same mosque. Likewise, the increasingly frequent eruption in Toronto of gang war, sometimes accompanied by murder, is always reported without any indication that the perpetrators tend to be Jamaican or members of other visible minorities who have introduced their gang culture to Canada.

Failure to reveal essential information about these events is no doubt prompted partly by the wish to forestall a dangerous backlash. But it also results from the desire to avoid casting ethnic minorities in an unfavourable light. It accords with Canada's amiable image. But it is profoundly counterproductive. Readiness to perform criminal or socially disruptive acts arises from very serious social and psychological problems embedded in the perpetrators' milieu, problems that are not likely to be confronted if they are concealed or brushed from view.

OF HOCKEY AND HUCKSTERS

One of my quibbles about Canada is so picayune, eccentric and profoundly un-Canadian that I blush to mention it. But the truth must out. I find the current form of the beloved national game unattractive and unacceptable. The antithesis of sport, it is a mean business in which obscenely huge rewards are paid for loutish behaviour. Remember Todd Bertuzzi—he who despite having gratuitously crippled an opposing player who was nowhere near the puck, was subsequently chosen by the saintly Wayne Gretzky to play on the Canadian team in the 2006 Winter Olympics? Remember the inevitable, boring fights every Saturday night? There is, admittedly, skill and sometimes grace in hockey, and excitement, but how can an otherwise gentle land elevate this commercialized mayhem into a revered national passion? How can we allow it to influence much of the leisure time of the country's male youth? How can so many otherwise responsible, serious and upstanding citizens be duped by this profit-driven commerce and fall for the wiles of a brutal industry?

One ought not, of course, to paint the whole edifice with the NHL brush. Large numbers of kids still chase a puck on the nearby pond mythologized in our folklore or, more likely, are ferried by frazzled hockey mums at ungodly hours to heavily booked arenas. Hockey, uncorrupted by market-driven roughness, is a fun game. Witness women's hockey, in which body checks—let alone punch-outs—are not permitted. Unfortunately, however, the sport's essential innocence, particularly insofar as youngsters are concerned, is increasingly tainted by its organizational side, which resists only with difficulty the values and practices of the industry.

Hockey insidiously seeps into the nooks and crannies of national life. An intriguing and disconcerting example is illustrated by a rather ill-conceived initiative of the CBC. It was, by the way, borrowed from the BBC in the UK. The Corporation launched a project in 2004 to select, by vote, a Canadian who had the most profound impact on the country's history. It was called the Greatest Canadian contest, as if such a choice were possible. There are many greatnesses and they cannot be compared. Very few women were nominated and the program was only conducted on the English service, so most Quebeckers were excluded. About 1.2 million votes were cast. Tommy Douglas, the CCF premier of Saskatchewan, widely seen as the father of medicare, came first, followed by Terry Fox, Pierre Trudeau, Frederick Banting, David Suzuki and Lester Pearson in sixth place. Who, do you suppose, came next, *ahead* of Sir John A. Macdonald and Alexander Graham Bell? Seventh place was occupied by none other than Don Cherry, the xenophobic, anti-French, violence-defending, loose-mouthed commentator on CBC's *Hockey Night in Canada*. He is popular among many hockey fans, but what has he contributed to Canada, other than a colourful and, to many—including me—decidedly unpalatable character exercising what I see as an unacceptable influence on the national game? Is this what the Peaceable Kingdom has come to?

In being influenced by the highly commercialized ethos of its surrounding society, hockey epitomizes a deeply distressing contemporary feature of Canada. If I were to rank the concerns I have about our collective judgement and future, I would place it at the top or very near to it. An exaggerated preoccupation with the bottom line, which is just another way of depicting this ill, is not, of course, a uniquely Canadian characteristic. It is a central aspect of a number of related phenomena linked to capitalism and its youngest child, globalization. No country is immune to it or would wish to be. But there are degrees to which life is infused with its materialistic and competitive preoccupations. And countries, utilizing the tools available to the state and the voluntary sector, are capable, to some measure, of defining the boundaries between economic and other spheres. Canada, largely because it is so vulnerable to American culture, has been slack and hence ineffective in resisting the worldwide trend. Economic criteria are all too often allowed to displace other, more fundamental priorities.

I already mentioned an area in which this *insouciance* is particularly noticeable and harmful: our willingness, sometimes even eagerness, to open our economy, and so our homeland, to foreign influence and takeovers. There are numerous other examples. One of them is the contemporary tendency to allow private, often egotistical, interests to invade the public sphere. Many needs and amenities that used to be available free as a public service must now be paid for, including some medical and social services, access to cultural and heritage sites and events, or scenic outdoor attractions. Even essential school supplies must increasingly be provided by parents, and littered highways are begging to be adopted by their users. Recreational spaces are less and less being treed using money from public funds. One runs the risk, nowadays, when stepping into a park, of stumbling over a newly planted sapling provided by a private donor to commemorate a departed relative or friend.

Privatization and user fees have become the slogans of our age. Few moments in our lives escape the onslaught of commercialism and commercialization. Can you think of any sports event—amateur or professional—whose players and sites have escaped being plastered with brazen or tacit advertising? Even cultural shrines, such as the Stratford Festival, become colossal billboards recognizing corporate or private donors. No part of its real estate escapes being named, including the trees and seemingly every blade of grass. The swans alone, when I last checked, were spared.

Only a twit would wish to knock individual and company generosity and support for good causes; it deserves to be applauded and recognized. But the growing need for it and its importance and prevalence attest to the shrinking of the public spheres—and the expansion of the private. Shared collective initiatives and concerns, which strengthen a sense of community, give way to private and individual action. The principal and potentially most capable champion of whole communities—the state—recedes into the background, making way for the market. It, by definition, pursues not some public good, but merely private gain.

Under these conditions, business values come to outweigh other, less materialistic considerations. Aesthetics, ethics, protection of the environment and of heritage structures and institutions, pure science, humane social arrangements for the less fortunate, disinterested long-term planning for neighbourhoods and communities, even just common garden-variety decency all suffer and give way to the crushing appetite of Mammon.

There is no way Canada can completely escape all of the byproducts of modern capitalism permeating the western world. But means exist to limit their effects. Some of them are even emerging within the business community itself. The Scandinavian countries, with respect to certain of these ills, others as well, have shown themselves capable of resisting or modifying the trend, and of achieving a greater creative harmony than we have between the interests of the market and the public good. North America lags far behind here and, regrettably, Canada, with the possible exception of Quebec, in this context is completely North American. Once again, it seems that our easygoing, cork-in-the-stream ways and our penchant for the path of least resistance lead us to go along with practices we ought to have the wit and gumption to reject. Here, too, therefore, laudable qualities turn out to have a down side.

The task of appraising a country is at least as daunting as that of a flea trying to build a skyscraper. The scope of the topic is immense and its complexities infinite. In coming to grips with a few salient Canadian features, space constraints have forced me to oversimplify, neglect qualifications, overlook relevant facts and nuances, and select examples rather than provide complete descriptions. As a result, one may well wonder to what extent the emerging picture represents something like objective reality and to what degree it is a self-portrait of the observer.

As I read over what has emerged in this chapter, it dawned on me that I was writing as much about myself as about the country. The features I find noteworthy, and how I see them, say a lot about what is important to me and where I stand. And I am startled to find that the emerging witness seems to be as much European as North American.

I see myself as totally Canadian. After all, I have lived in Canada for more than sixty years, have exhaustively studied it, became involved in many of its causes, represented it at innumerable international meetings and have passionately identified with it. The vast majority of my students—one of the principal preoccupations and joys of my adult life—were Canadians steeped in the country's essence. I could not but be imbued with their world. Although I like a lot about Europe and visit regularly, as I noted, I do not feel part of it and much prefer to live in Canada.

Earlier, I drew some comparisons between Canada and Austria, favourable to the latter. What I did not mention, because it was irrelevant in the context, was that although I admire its defence of the national identity, I also harbour criticisms of Austria, some of which are quite severe. Austria's reaction to Hitler and Nazism was reprehensible, and its postwar failure to confront past errors (as Germany has done) even more so. The country, pretending that it was a victim of German aggression, has never come clean. By comparison, Canada's shortcomings with respect to Chinese and Jewish immigrants or its aboriginal population are nowhere near the Austrian lapse of humanity and candour.

But let us return to our sheep, as the French say. Many of the reactions recorded here seem to have their roots in Old World culture and even in the Social Democratic values of my youth. These appear to have partially survived as guideposts to the identification of society's ills, although they no longer offer sure prescriptions for redress, as they once did.

When it comes to drawing up the balance sheet between the *"j'accuse"* and the *"j'adore"* ledgers heralded in this chapter's title, the latter wins hands down. Among the foibles of *Homo sapiens* is that we tend to be most demanding and exacting with respect to those closest to us. We demand more from family members and other loved ones than we do from strangers. It is well to keep this in mind while confronting my criticism of Canada. Perhaps because I am so very fond of the place and so much part of it, in weighing its virtues and failings, I may have set the bar a bit too high. But if my judgement is a mite harsh, I have no regrets. Dissatisfaction and disappointment can serve as useful inducements—to oneself and others—for a greater and more effective effort to help Canada live up to its potential.

ENVOI

Discovering how European I remain and uncovering my bizarre reaction to organized hockey are just two examples of the surprises that awaited me when I began writing my memoirs and opened this particular Pandora's box of national identity. A great many other Canadians probably carry in themselves to varying degrees vestiges of national and other group characteristics and qualities that affect their outlook and of which they are unaware. Other essayists in this book, prodded and poked by Janice Stein's challenge, have had to think their way through this labyrinth as well. I hope they will agree with me that it is well worth the journey.

Prime Minister John Diefenbaker used to make much of his displeasure with the practice common in the 1950s and '60s of referring to Canadians as German Canadians, Chinese Canadians or what have you. Shaking his jowls alarmingly, he would inveigh against the use of what he referred to as "hyphenated Canadians." We were all just Canadians and qualifying adjectives were, to him, highly offensive. That is exactly what I saw in myself. I was your prototypical *un*-hyphenated Canadian. I had fully internalized, I thought, the prevailing outlook of what I took to be mainstream, responsible and public-spirited English-speaking Canadians. I had studied and experienced *la grande difference* between those English speakers and the country's francophones and rejoiced in it, just as I recognized and respected that various ethnic minorities maintained some of the traditions and values of their forebears. A few groups tended to dwell unrealistically on certain historical wrongs or crimes, but *c'est la vie*. It did not alter their status as Canadians. Now I wonder whether, unbeknownst to me, I have all along been a Czech Canadian, a Euro-Canadian or perhaps a Central European Canadian.

The latent or unperceived residue in an immigrant's psyche is of critical importance in understanding Canadian multiculturalism. It attests to the presence in many of us of ethnic legacies of which we are unaware. The free, unattached, soaring spirit I imagined myself to be turns out to be a traveller with baggage.

❦ ❦ ❦

It has been one of my foibles to conclude even my most academic or number-crunching papers, whenever possible, with some normative thoughts arising from the research. So, inevitably I ask, is there anything we can learn from the foregoing ruminations? Among various possibilities, I alight on only one lesson, perhaps a bit paradoxically (Janus again?) and inappropriately in the present context.

Despite its undoubted critical salience in Canadian life, I wonder whether some Canadians have allowed the multicultural nature of their country to preoccupy them *too much*. Numerically these people are a minority, but they generate a lot of buzz. Some are "professional ethnics" who make a good thing out of their origin and so assiduously perpetuate differences; others are obsessed by ethnic issues to the exclusion of almost everything else. Some members of the latter group fall into this category only intellectually. Their background is *pukka*, WASPish old establishment, but their feeling of collective guilt and bleeding-heart disposition lead them to sacrifice other priorities to an accommodation of extreme multiculturalism.

At least two consequences of an over-emphasis on our heterogeneity bother me. The first is that it may deflect the political process from addressing other, equally or more pressing problems such as First Nations needs and health care. The other is substantive: meeting the needs of global humanity (environmental issues, an arms race in space, genetic manipulation) must, in my book, take precedence over satisfying specific groups, whether they be ethnic, religious or geographic.

It is all too easy—but harmful—to forget that in a democracy like ours innumerable interests have to be accommodated, and ethnic concerns compete with others for attention. Historically, issues arising from the population's varied backgrounds were woefully neglected.

Redress was needed, and to a very great extent it has occurred. Multiculturalism has become an accepted counter in the vast game of collective decision making in Canada. More needs to be done and, as this volume indicates, a number of issues related to it still need to be addressed. But we are well on the way.

There are those who believe that certain matters, such as questions of faith and religious or long-term secular practice, outweigh others in importance because they arise from absolute truths. Some see them as sacrosanct. Others, however, lack this faith and cling with equal fervour to other and contrary verities. Who is to say what is right in a greatly mixed society? The answer depends on the nature of the final authority on which norms rest. Is it divine, a social contract, an immemorial custom, a ruler, majority opinion or what? Theologians and philosophers have grappled with these and related conundrums for thousands of years without, so far, arriving at a consensus acceptable to everyone. Under these circumstances, the only tolerable way, in a peaceful, civil society, is to accept the uncomfortable, often messy process of engaging in the politics of accommodation, which involves tolerating compromises and unpalatable decisions, getting less than one hoped for and resigning oneself to living in an imperfect world. For a great many good souls these are exceedingly hard things to live with. The more central to one's life and the more emotionally loaded the matter, the more difficult accommodation becomes.

In the domains explored in this volume—multiculturalism, individual and group rights, practices and values idiosyncratic to some but bothersome to others, making "newcomers" feel comfortable without unduly bothering "old settlers" and vice versa, honouring the Charter but not abusing it, interpreting the Charter sensitively—in all these areas, decisions and practices that prove widely acceptable can only emerge as the result of the application and acceptance of the give-and-take characteristic of democratic politics. The latter and the politics of multiculturalism are inextricably intertwined.

Because these matters often involve profoundly felt values and concerns that are deemed to surpass ordinary human or merely personal dimensions, they are sometimes endowed with special characteristics. These are expected by some to override normal processes. But it is precisely because of their huge significance and centrality in human lives that they cannot be treated as exceptions but must be governed by universal rules and conventions applicable to all.

The success, therefore, of multiculturalism in any specific setting depends to a very great extent on the quality and legitimacy of the overall political system. Anyone wishing to enhance multiculturalism depends on the health of the democratic system as a whole.

Seismic Tremors: Religion and the Law

Michael Valpy

Late in 2006, I took part in a conference in Ireland on the role that the media plays in the evolution of new national identities.[1] One of the speakers, a leading Irish journalist, declared at the outset of his presentation that "we don't want the horror story of Canada," referring to our 250-year-old wobbly, stressful dialectic between francophones and anglophones plus our more recent testy bouts of flailing in the multicultural fog. It is useful to learn about how others see us, even—or especially—when they inhabit a culture where some months earlier a report of Protestants getting together with Roman Catholics in a small town in Ulster to jointly assault Russian immigrants was wryly deemed an advance of the 1998 peace plan.

Canada viewed as a multicultural horror story is something most of its inhabitants would find odd. David Cameron writes that this country, except for its miserable failure to live honourably with aboriginal peoples—a big "except"—has done a pretty good job of managing diversity, learned in the quest for accommodation between its two great linguistic communities. "Had we not been forced to struggle, since our very beginnings, with the existential reality of cultural dualism," says Cameron, "we would not have been nearly so well equipped to adapt ourselves and our society to cultural pluralism."

Nonetheless, in the two-pronged thesis Janice Gross Stein has set down for this book, the horizon has fat, dark clouds. Religion—one of the most powerful elements of culture—is accosting our normative values, intensified by the global rise of religious orthodoxies. And contemporary newcomers to Canada and their offspring are not strolling into the mainstream with anywhere near the élan of past immigrant cohorts; increasingly they see themselves isolated and identified as the Other rather than slipping effortlessly into the warm bath of the Canadian ethos. Those two issues, religion and immigration, are often, of course, linked: our commitment to freedom of religion grows out of the value we place on diversity and multiculturalism, and, as Stein observes, many immigrants to Canada bring with them a commitment to religious practice so deep that, for them, religion is inseparable from culture.

It is also important to point out that these multicultural bumps Canadians are encountering are being felt elsewhere, and with greater intensity than what is mildly, so far, rattling our teeth at home. Stuart Soroka, Richard Johnston and Keith Banting (2007), in their essay "Ties That Bind? Social Cohesion and Diversity in Canada," note that growing ethnic diversity has generated two intersecting policy agendas throughout the western democracies—one celebrating diversity and the other focusing on social cohesion and social integration. In the last quarter of the twentieth century, say the authors, many western democracies embraced an accommodating approach to ethnic diversity, adopting a wide range of programs designed to extend some level of public recognition and support for ethnocultural minorities to maintain and express their distinct identities and practices. "With a few notable exceptions, this more multiculturalist approach represented the dominant trend in Western democracies in the closing decades of the last century. In the first decade of this new century, the balance of debate is shifting again. There is renewed concern about social integration in diverse societies"—an observation affirmed by the fact we have written this book.

Thus in countries such as France, Germany, Australia, the Netherlands, the United States, Britain and elsewhere, governments are moving to supplement multicultural programs with nation-building or integrationist measures, and social analysts are writing about a retreat from multiculturalism and the return of assimilation. Until recently, say

Soroka, Johnston and Banting, "these debates have had limited resonance in Canada, and Canadians have often been puzzled by the intensity of debates elsewhere." But no more. The northern kingdom is
still peaceable, the lion lying with the lamb, but rumblings are beginning to be heard—and what these rumblings should tell us is this:
first, that we have no grounds for smugness or complacency about the
state of our multiculturalism; second, that however well we may have
done in the past in effecting multiculturalism-lite, the mosey is over,
and what lies ahead is multiculturalism-tough.

Multiculturalism-lite is having a colour-blind immigration policy
and a good and sensitive public school system and telling ourselves we
have created a flexible, tolerant and inclusive society. All of which we
have accomplished, more or less, and yet we are not skipping down the
path to a post-ethnic identity that I and other public commentators
have written wishfully about (Anderssen and Valpy 2004).

It is a big step from the value of tolerance of newcomers who are
different—a value that Canadians by and large embrace and exercise—to the value of acceptance, which we still fall short of. A big step
from a culture of legal equality to one of social equality. A big step
from closed patterns of association, from the social distancing between most ethnic groups that is the norm in Canada to building community that crosses ethnic lines. Contrary to our national mythology,
we never deliberately invented the multicultural mosaic as an alternative to the American melting pot. Rather, as Cameron writes, "the
preservation of migrant origin and identity has been more of an option north of the forty-ninth parallel than south." (So much has come
easily to us.) What lies ahead must be awareness that if our multicultural mosaic is meant to be a structural feature of Canadian society, it
indeed needs to have an impact on power relations and, ultimately,
on the core cultural character of the society. It needs to truly alter national identity. It would be an affront to our publicly cherished values
to wall out any more of our fellow citizens than we do already from the
Canadian dream, especially those whose skin is not white. It is dis-
graceful enough that we do it to the poor and aboriginals.

An underreported comment made by Toronto mayor David Miller
in the 2006 municipal election campaign was his declaration that

Canada's largest city is not immune to the factors that ignited the *ban-lieu* riots in France by disaffected visible minority youth (*Now* magazine 2006). The statement has been dismissed as an exaggeration, but I am not sure it should be.

Since the 1980s, Canada's immigration narrative has been different from the past: the country has opened its doors to hundreds upon hundreds of thousands of people whose home cultures are far removed from the mainstream culture of Canada. Beneath the patina of welcome and tolerance, many newcomers have come to see themselves as victims of discrimination and alienation. Despite high levels of education and training, they are faring worse in the labour market than earlier migrants to Canada. They are living more and more in segregated residential areas. And it is their children—the second generation, either born in Canada or raised in Canada from childhood—who are the greatest cause for concern. Canada is the only country this new generation knows. Canada is their home. Yet an alarmingly significant percentage of them feel even less welcome and more alienated than their parents, less able than their parents to pass through the cultural veils into mainstream Canada. They don't feel accepted in Canada, don't understand its values and don't feel Canadian.

What the data show—from Statistics Canada's 2002 Ethnic Diversity Survey and other studies, and analyzed by scholars such as University of Toronto sociologist Jeffrey Reitz, one of Canada's foremost experts on multiculturalism, and the Institute for Research on Public Policy—is a generation raised in the rhetorical milieu of both multiculturalism and the Canadian Charter of Rights and Freedoms, young people who expect to be treated as equals in Canadian society and who are discovering angrily that they are not (Reitz and Banerjee 2007). Their disaffection has gone largely unnoticed until now in polls and academic research because, unlike in France, the numbers of the visible-minority second generation are statistically small—less than a million. If they are a sign of things to come, we've got troubles. Because, as Reitz states, "it is striking that indications of lack of integration into Canadian society are so significant for second-generation minorities, since they are regarded as the harbinger of the future."

Striking, but to many social agency workers in the field, not surprising. Years of relentless government spending cutbacks in education support programs—arts and cultural instruction, after-school engagement and social work and psychological services—and in community and immigrant settlement services have increasingly left newcomer families on their own, and walled into ethnic enclaves.

The data show that, for the immigrant second generation, all visible minorities have less of a sense of belonging to the country than do whites. On virtually all indicators used by sociologists and governments to measure integration into Canadian life, visible minorities rate themselves as less integrated than whites. Add their perceptions of non-belonging to their socioeconomic rankings—among all ethnocultural groups in Canada, racial minorities clearly have the lowest relative household income and the highest poverty rates—and the outlines of underclass loom menacingly out of the mist.

We would also be foolhardy to ignore the most recent research of Harvard political scientist Robert Putnam of *Bowling Alone* fame. In the largest ever study of "civic engagement" in America—26,200 people in 40 US communities—Putnam concluded that the more people of different races lived in the same community, the greater the loss of trust. Those in highly diverse communities "don't trust the local mayor, they don't trust the local paper, they don't trust other people and they don't trust institutions," said Putnam. "The only thing there's more of is protest marches and TV-watching" (Shipman 2006). Indeed, Putnam told a Manchester University audience that, counterintuitively, "the effect of diversity is worse than had been imagined. And it's not just that we don't trust people who are not like us. In diverse communities, we don't trust people who do look like us."

Those are American rather than Canadian findings, and the societal chemistry south of the border is different. Nevertheless, many of the ingredients are the same, and Putnam considered his research results so explosive that for half a decade he didn't dare announce them.

I do not want a Canada that turns its back on multiculturalism. Nor do I want a Canada of white elites and disaffected brown, black and yellow people. I do not want a Canada where, not unrelatedly, citizenship is looked upon as a mere flag of convenience by hundreds of thousands, even millions, who qualify for passports but do not consider Canada as home. I am not ready for a Canada that is merely—in the phrase of novelist Yann Martel—"the greatest hotel on earth."[2] Let me echo Janice Stein and say that there are conversations we need to have.

We have always been a political nationality, never bonded by blood or tribe, as George-Étienne Cartier said of Canadians-to-be in 1865. That means we have always needed visible signs of our togetherness — primarily, as is the case with nationalities like ours, signs crafted by the state. And yet concomitantly with the in-migration of people with languages and cultures increasingly distant from the languages and culture of the Canadian mainstream, the visible symbols of Canada have been eroding as the state retreats from our lives — the result, *inter alia*, of continuing decentralization so that we're expected now to be Quebeckers, Albertans and Ontarians ahead of being Canadians; the result of a halt to the creation of new national social programs and an end to anything resembling an activist and altruistic foreign policy; the result of once publicly owned corporations such as Air Canada, Canadian National Railways and Petro-Canada being privatized by a succession of neo-liberal governments or, like the Canadian Broadcasting Corporation, emasculated, all with no perceivable benefit to the common good and no new creations in nation building to take their place. Bernard Ostry, the late, great mandarin of the federal public service who crafted Canada's multicultural policy in the 1970s, stressed in the last years before his death in 2006 that multiculturalism was urgently in need of being placed under the microscope of a royal commission and having its contemporary state and its impact on Canadian life thoroughly examined.

I am a journalist, not a social scientist or a politician. I don't have the expertise to propose what nuts, bolts and girders are necessary to build and maintain an organic, lively, participatory society. Charles Taylor says social identity is derived from an agreement on the common goods of society, and he defines some of those goods as "hypergoods" from which all our normative positions are judged and the articulation of which provide "a necessary condition of adhesion" (Taylor 1990, 27). Those hypergoods are the common cultural values for us all — our uniculture — and, like David Cameron, I believe that the threads of uniculturalism must underlie and sustain the quilt of multiculturalism, and that without social cohesion, our democracy is blunted, along with our expressions of public policy such as health care, education, the arts, environmental protection, individual rights and the conduct of our foreign affairs. There is stuff the market can't do. If we don't feel we are together, we don't work to build things together.

So that is the first *tranche*, a reflection on Canadians who find themselves outside the ethos of being Canadian. The second *tranche* is about religion.

The question Janice Stein raises, looking at current events around her and her experience in her own Toronto synagogue, is what we do when religious teaching and practice contradict the seminal values of Canadian society—the hypergoods, if you like—respecting the autonomy, dignity and equality of individuals, specifically of women and homosexuals. Chief Justice Beverley McLachlin (2004, 14) of Canada has called this the fundamental tension of Canadian society.

Canada has no constitutional doctrine of separation of church and state. Religious institutions are exempted by governments from paying property taxes. They are designated as charities, thus financial contributions made to them qualify for tax credits. In most provinces, religious schools receive public funds and, in Ontario, the Roman Catholic school system is fully funded by government from Grades 1 to 12. All of this may—*may*—be interpreted as the state's imprimatur being stamped on their activities.

Sociologists of religion tend to include this country in the faith desert that sweeps across western Europe, a characterization that is mostly but not entirely accurate. We are a far more secular society than our neighbours to the south. Only about 20 percent of Canadians regularly attend religious services, despite roughly 85 percent claiming adherence to a specific faith, a claim that demographers and record keepers of various religious organizations know to be grossly inflated. Still, there are religious hotspots in both Atlantic and western Canada, and frequent attendance at religious institutions is actually inching upward in our three largest cities. The latter phenomenon is entirely because of immigration, and religious attendance by the second generation of immigrant families quickly comes to resemble the stay-away attendance patterns of the larger native-born population— although there are blips of exception.

What the statistics do not adequately reflect is the rising presence and vocality in Canada of religious orthodoxy, a startling global development that has touched all of the world's major religions, most notably the three Abrahamic faiths of Judaism, Christianity and Islam.

The British author Karen Armstrong, whose scholarly books on religion sell in the millions, has written that all "fundamentalist" forms of religion follow a certain pattern:

> They are embattled forms of spirituality, which have emerged as a response to a perceived crisis. They are engaged in a conflict with enemies whose secularist policies and beliefs seem inimical to religion itself. Fundamentalists do not regard this battle as a conventional political struggle, but experience it as a cosmic war between the forces of good and evil.... This religious resurgence has taken many observers by surprise. In the middle years of the twentieth century, it was generally taken for granted that secularism was an irreversible trend and that faith would never again play a major part in world events. It was assumed that as human beings became more rational, they either would have no further need for religion or would be content to confine it to the immediately personal and private areas of their lives. But in the late 1970s, fundamentalists began to rebel against this secularist hegemony and started to wrest religion out of its marginal position and back to center stage. In this, at least, they have enjoyed remarkable success. Religion has once again become a force that no government can safely ignore. Fundamentalism has suffered defeats, but it is by no means quiescent. It is now an essential part of the modern scene and will certainly play an important role in the domestic and international affairs of the future. (Armstrong 2000, pp. xiii, xi–xii)

In an interview with *The Globe and Mail*, Ms. Armstrong said the reason religious fundamentalism exists is that it is the natural byproduct of a secular, liberal society. "So to every [secular advance of] society, there is a fundamentalist riposte. We have to be grown-up about it. All major social change is contested. It always has been. Not everyone is going to say, 'Oh boy, what a fabulous idea, let's go along with it.'" In particular, she said, the emancipation of women has fuelled fundamentalism in all major religions, and Christianity has been "the worst religion in the world for integrating sexuality and gender with the sacred" (Valpy 2004).

Religious orthodoxy's presence in Canada treads with a lighter step than in most parts of the world and certainly falls short of what recently has been described in the United States as "the biggest political and cultural movement of our times" (Sharlet 2006). But it is here and it is making itself known. It has fought the political battle against legalization of same-sex marriage, defended politicians who publicly denounce homosexuality and attempted to control the legal mechanisms applying to assisted human reproduction.

The Roman Catholic church continues to discriminate against women in employment by not ordaining them as priests. It considers homosexuality a "disordered" condition—and presumably teaches this to students in its school system, one of whom was required to get a court order to permit him to take his gay date to his high school graduation prom. Yet as former Supreme Court justice Claire L'Heureux-Dubé has observed, "there can no longer be any doubt that sexual orientation discrimination in education violates deeply and widely accepted views of elementary justice."[3] The church opposed, along with a number of other religious organizations, legislation permitting same-sex marriage, while more than one of its bishops mused aloud about excommunicating Catholic members of Parliament who voted in favour of the legislation despite Canadian Revenue Agency rules that prohibit charitable organizations—including churches—from engaging in partisan political activity and strictly regulate the amount of time they can devote to political lobbying. It has fired teachers who remarried without getting their first marriages annulled by the church, and it has forced gay teachers out of employment.

The Anglican Church of Canada, to which I belong, discriminates against homosexuals in employment by forbidding its gay priests to be sexually active. At the time of this writing, it has been unable to bring itself to officially approve the blessing of same-sex unions, let alone the solemnization of same-sex marriages, citing issues of "scriptural interpretation" and "church unity" (but not "homophobia").

In Quebec, Canada's most secular province, a plethora of religious incidents has publicly surfaced. A Montreal YMCA agreed to install frosted windows in one of its exercise rooms to "accommodate" a neighbouring Hasidic school that wanted to prevent its teenaged male students from looking at women in workout gear. A downtown Montreal YWCA invited parents to observe their children's swimming lesson. But, because of a mix-up in the schedule, it turned out that a group of Muslim women was having a water aerobic session in another part of the pool; they demanded that all men, including fathers watching their kids swimming, be excluded from the pool area. The YWCA complied. At a community clinic, men accompanying their spouses to prenatal classes were sent away because Muslim women objected to their presence. At a medical clinic, an Orthodox Jew was allowed to see the doctor instantly, bypassing patients who had been waiting for their turn, because he argued that he had to be home before the Sabbath (which starts at sunset). In other instances, Quebec health practitioners have reported having to deal with fundamentalist Muslims who refuse to let male nurses or doctors touch their wives even though they may be gravely ill and there is no available female professional in the ward. According to a recent survey done for *La Presse* and *Le Soleil*, six out of ten Quebeckers think society has gone too far down the road of *accommodement raisonnable* [reasonable accommodation] of religious groups, a view interestingly that is more prevalent among people with higher levels of education and income. Yet the same survey showed that most respondents (68.1 percent) consider immigration to be an asset for Quebec (Gagnon 2007).

In Ontario, only after strong public protest that the constitutional equality rights of women were at risk of being undermined did the provincial government back away from a previous decision allowing religious institutions to operate under provincial arbitration legislation to impose divorce and child custody settlements on families under religious laws—e.g., sharia for Muslims; the rabbinical beit din courts for Jews—that could not be reviewed by the secular courts.

Rather paradoxically, today's faith leaders declare that they are involuntarily marginalized in the public sphere, kept off the public stage for solemn moments in the nation's life and largely ignored by the news media except when they say something outrageous or highly controversial or are required to answer for some institutional scandal.

As Claude Ryan (2004, ix), the late journalist, politician and, for nearly twenty years, national secretary of Quebec's Action catholique, said in a lecture at McGill University in 2002:

> There has been a tendency since World War II to relegate religion to the private sphere; to suggest that it should have as little as possible to do with economic, social, and political life. This approach appeared to succeed for a time. But religion, in my opinion, cannot be confined indefinitely to the private sphere.... It is possible in principle to make distinctions between those things that belong to the temporal order and those that pertain to the spiritual order, but in practice—in actual relations between human beings—that is not the way the problem poses itself.

The issue should be framed a little differently. It is not the participation of religious institutions in the public sphere that is a problem. The problem is public support for faith institutions—through tax credits and funded schools—that in their teaching and practice denigrate the constitutional rights of women and homosexuals while claiming constitutional protection for themselves under freedom of religion and conscience.

One illustration:

In 2002, 17-year-old Marc Hall, a Grade 12 student at Monsignor John Pereyma Catholic School in the Durham Catholic District School Board just east of Toronto, sought permission from his principal to bring his boyfriend as his date to his graduation prom and was refused.

School trustees at first denied him the opportunity to speak to the board, but subsequently relented in the face of public and media criticism and then voted unanimously to support the principal's decision. Although Mr. Hall was ostensibly protected by both the Charter and Ontario human rights legislation against discrimination on the grounds of his sexual orientation and had the constitutional right of freedom of association, Durham Catholic Board chair Mary Ann Martin declared that "the homosexual lifestyle goes against the teachings of the church and we support that. We have the right in the Catholic school system to protect our rights and beliefs" (Josey 2002). And church

spokesperson Suzanne Scorsone, normally a paragon of political as-
tuteness and sensitivity, declared that criticism of the board's decision raised the spectre of religious intolerance against Catholics. "People have a choice as to whether they attend a Catholic school or not,"
she said. "There are other options available to them, and for people to
choose to be practising Catholics ... [is to] acknowledge the rightness
of the teachings themselves" (Brean 2002). The teachings being that
homosexuality is a disordered condition. The board's lawyer, Peter
Lauwers, declared: "Catholic schools are about indoctrination. They
are about inculcating the faith. We're about indoctrination plain and
simple" (Barber 2002). The Roman Catholic bishop responsible for the
Durham region said the school prom to which Mr. Hall wanted to take
his boyfriend had "denominational content" that would protect it from
state interference (Kari 2002).

Mr. Hall sought an injunction from the Ontario Superior Court of
Justice to block the school board's action. And at the hearing before Mr.
Justice Robert MacKinnon, one of Hall's lawyers, Douglas Elliot, put the
essence of his case: "Archbishop Ambrozic [Cardinal Aloysius Ambrozic, archbishop of Toronto] can stand up in the pulpit in the cathedral and say Marc Hall and all people like him are going to burn in Hell
for eternity, and no one would suggest that he should ever be stopped
from saying that. But when Archbishop Ambrozic accepts the Queen's
shilling, he has to take the Queen's terms. If he doesn't like those terms
then he can refuse the cheque" (Barber 2002).

Justice MacKinnon ruled that the board's right to inculcate religious views does not override Mr. Hall's human rights. "If individuals
in Canada were permitted to simply assert that their religious beliefs
require them to discriminate against homosexuals, without objective
scrutiny, there would be no protection at all from discrimination for
gays and lesbians in Canada because everyone who wished to discriminate against them could make that assertion" (Oziewicz 2002).
He said the board's decision to prohibit Mr. Hall from attending the
prom with his boyfriend was "an unjustified breach" of section 15
equality rights. "The idea of equality rights speaks to the conscience
of all humanity—the dignity and the worth that is due each human
being," Justice MacKinnon wrote. "Marc Hall is a Roman Catholic Cana-

dian trying to be himself. He is gay. It is not an answer to his section 15 Charter rights, on these facts, to deny him permission to attend his school's function with his classmates in order to celebrate his high school career."

School board chairwoman Mary Ann Martin called the decision "totally wrong" (Kalinowski 2002).

Just reflect on what she said: It is "totally wrong" for a government body, Ontario's publicly funded Roman Catholic school system, to be told that it cannot prohibit a teenager—whose rights to equality and freedom of association are protected by Canada's Constitution—from taking his boyfriend to a school dance.

And reflect on what University of Toronto religious philosopher David Novak had to say. He called Justice MacKinnon's ruling "an assault on the integrity of every religious community in Canada" (Fulford 2002). He told an international conference on religious freedom at British Columbia's Christian evangelical Trinity Western University that "every activity of a Catholic school should be recognizably Catholic, just as every activity of a Jewish school should be recognizably Jewish." He said that the Durham Catholic school board "has as much right to determine who may attend its social activities and how he or she may attend them as it has the right to teach Catholic theology in its religion classes as authoritative teaching. *It should not be left to the final decision of any particular human court*" (Todd 2002, italics added).

There are fascinating issues raised here. And let me make clear that, in attempting to address them, I am not embarking on an anti-religious screed. My values were shaped by western Canada's Protestant Social Gospel. But I suggest that among the difficult conversations Canadians are in need of having is whether religion is one of the hypergoods of Canada. Is it part of Canadian uniculture? What are the limits to protecting freedom of religion in a liberal democratic society? Should the state support religious institutions that practice or advocate discrimination against women or homosexuals? Is there a rationale in a multicultural liberal democratic society for publicly funded religious schools regardless of historic constitutional protection? Is the Canada that cemented religious school rights into its constitution in the mid-nineteenth century the same Canada that has seventeen-year-old Marc Hall wanting to take his boyfriend to a school graduation dance at the beginning of the twenty-first century? And if we don't know the answers to those questions, isn't it time we started to find them?

Chief Justice McLachlin has gone in search of the answers, and, in a thoughtful, sensitive and careful lecture on freedom of religion and the rule of law, delivered at McGill in 2002, she presents a portrait of two world views on an inevitable collision course, and what to do when they smack into one another.

To limn the rule of law, she turns to Yale's Paul Kahn, who explains that "there is no part of modern life to which law does not extend.... The rule of law shapes our experience of meaning everywhere and at all times. It is not alone in shaping meaning, but it is rarely absent" (Kahn 1999, 123, 124, quoted in McLachlin 2004, 14). The chief justice continues in her own words: "Voting, taxation, mobility, family organization, and public discourse: the rule of law leaves no aspect of human experience unaffected by its claim to authority" (McLachlin 2004, 14).

But as much as the rule of law makes total claims upon the self, it is also, in Kahn's words, "a way of being in the world that must compete with other forms of social and political perception" (Kahn 1999, 84, quoted in McLachlin 2004, 14). Thus, as the chief justice says, "there are other sources of authority, other cultural modes of belief, that make strong claims upon the citizen" (McLachlin 2004, 14).

And so she turns to religion, and to the cultural anthropologist Clifford Geertz, who describes religion as "a cultural form that imbues all facets of the adherent's life and finds authority in transcendent principles" (Geertz 1973, quoted in McLachlin 2004, 15). "There are no limits to the claims made by religion upon the self," said McLachlin (2004, 15). "Religious authority, grounded as it is in basic assumptions about the nature of the cosmos, impinges upon all aspects of the adherent's world." In fact, the Supreme Court spoke of religion in *R. v. Edwards Books and Art Ltd.* (1986) as "profoundly personal beliefs that govern one's perception of oneself, humankind, nature and, in some cases, a higher or different order of being. These beliefs, in turn, govern one's conduct and practices."[4]

Which leaves us, very obviously, with the double *Weltanschauung.* "I wish," says the chief justice, "to call this tension between the rule of

law and the claims of religion 'a dialectic of normative commitments'"
(McLachlin 2004, 21).

How does the dialectic play out? I will end by quoting Chief Justice
McLachlin (2004, 16, 21) at length.

> [The] overarching demands of the rule of law and of religious con-
> science dramatize one of the foundational issues raised by the legal
> protection of freedom of religion.... [A] fundamental tenet of the rule
> of law is that all people are subject to its authority. It makes total
> claims upon the self and leaves little of human experience untouched.
> Yet religion exerts a similarly comprehensive claim. In the minds of
> adherents, its authority stands outside and above that of the law. So by
> examining freedom of religion, we are asking how one authoritative
> and ubiquitous system of cultural understanding—the rule of law—ac-
> commodates another similarly comprehensive system of belief. The
> modern religious citizen is caught between two all-encompassing sets
> of commitments. The law faces the seemingly paradoxical task of as-
> serting its own ultimate authority while carving out a space within
> itself in which individuals and communities can manifest alternate,
> and often competing, sets of ultimate commitments....
>
> What is good, true, and just in religion will not always comport with
> the law's view of the matter, nor will society at large always properly
> respect conscientious adherence to alternate authorities and divergent
> normative, or ethical, commitments. Where this is so, two comprehen-
> sive worldviews collide. It is at this point that the question of law's
> treatment of religion becomes truly exigent.

Let me underscore that point. When there's a clash, action is required, says the chief justice. Swift, decisive action.

> The rule of law presents itself as an authoritative force and, in a
> democracy, the content of this authority generally reflects majoritar-
> ian views and interests. For society to function properly it must be
> able to depend on some general consensus with respect to the norms
> that should be manifested in the law. The authority of the rule of law
> depends upon this. On the other hand, in Canadian society there is
> the value that we place upon multiculturalism and diversity, which
> brings with it a commitment to freedom of religion. But the beliefs
> and actions manifested when this freedom is granted can collide with

conventional legal norms. This clash of forces demands a resolution
from the courts. The reality of litigation means that cases must be resolved. The dialectic must reach synthesis. (MacLachlin 2004, 22)

Not the don't-touch-us response advocated by Rabbi Novak.
Preferably the politicians should give us synthesis, but failing that ...

The role of the courts, says Chief Justice McLachlin, is to place
markers in society's horizon of meaning, to explain what values are in-
comparably crucial to Canadian society, values that include human
dignity, autonomy and respect for the parallel rights of others.

She quotes her predecessor, Brian Dickson, who wrote in *R. v. Big
M Drug Mart Ltd.* (1985) that protection of religious freedom means
one is "free to hold and to manifest whatever beliefs and opinions his
or her conscience dictates, provided *inter alia* only that such manifestations do not injure his or her neighbours or their parallel rights
to hold and manifest beliefs and opinions of their own."[5]

Concludes Chief Justice McLachlin (2004, 31): "Freedom of religion, in this view, counsels both for the absence of coercion and respect
for the diversity of opinions." A notion I believe a loving God would embrace.

NOTES

1 The theme of the 2006 Anne Maguire Student Journalism Conference was
"New National Identities and the Role of the Media," organized by Co-op-
eration Ireland. See http://www.cooperationireland.org/?q=whatwedo/
media/2006conf (March 2007).
2 Martel says has been misunderstood, but the words speak for themselves.
3 *Trinity Western University v. College of Teachers*, [2001] 1 S.C.R. 772, 2001
SCC 31.
4 *R. v. Edwards Books and Art Ltd.*, [1986] 2 S.C.R. 713.
5 *R. v. Big M Drug Mart Ltd.*, [1985] 1 S.C.R. 295.

REFERENCES

Anderssen, Erin, and Michael Valpy et al. 2004. *The New Canada: A Globe
and Mail Report on the Next Generation*. Toronto: McClelland and
Stewart.
Armstrong, Karen. 2000. *The Battle for God*. New York: Knopf.

Barber, John. 2002. "Catholic Prom May Set Crucial Legal Precedent." *Globe and Mail*, May 9, p. A22.

Brean, Joseph. 2002. "Gay Acts 'Contrary to Natural Law.'" *National Post*, April 10, p. A08.

Fulford, Robert. 2002. "On Our List of Rights, Religion Comes Last." *National Post*, November 30, p. A27.

Gagnon, Lysiane. 2007. "How Far Must We Go to Do Right?" *Globe and Mail*, January 8, p. A15.

Geertz, Clifford. 1973. *The Interpretation of Cultures: Selected Essays*. New York: HarperCollins.

Josey, Stan. 2002. "Police Remove Student's Supporter—Durham Catholic Board Won't Discuss Gay Date to Prom." *Toronto Star*, March 26, p. B01.

Kahn, Paul. 1999. *The Cultural Study of Law: Reconstructing Legal Scholarship*. Chicago: University of Chicago Press. Cited in Beverley McLachlin. 2004. "Freedom of Religion and the Rule of Law: A Canadian Perspective." In Douglas Farrow, ed., *Recognizing Religion in a Secular Society: Essays in Pluralism, Religion and Public Policy*. Montreal and Kingston: McGill-Queen's University Press.

Kalinowski, Tess. 2002. "Student Drops Prom-Date Challenge." *Toronto Star*, June 29, p. B03.

Kari, Shannon. 2002. "School Is Violating Gay Teen's Rights—Lawyer." *Ottawa Citizen*, May 7, p. A4.

McLachlin, Beverley. 2004. "Freedom of Religion and the Rule of Law: A Canadian Perspective." In Douglas Farrow, ed., *Recognizing Religion in a Secular Society: Essays in Pluralism, Religion and Public Policy*. Montreal and Kingston: McGill-Queen's University Press.

Now. 2006. "Miller on the Grill." Vol. 26, no. 9. http://www.nowtoronto.com/issues/2006–11–02/news_story2.php (March 2007).

Oziewicz, Estanislao. 2002. "Supreme Court Challenge Looms Catholic School Board to Take Case to Trial after Judge Overturns Ban on Gay Prom Date." *Globe and Mail*, May 11, p. A10.

Reitz, Jeffrey, and Rupa Banerjee. 2007. "Racial Inequality, Social Cohesion and Policy Issues in Canada." In Keith Banting, Thomas J. Courchene and F. Leslie Seidle, eds., *Belonging? Diversity, Recognition and Shared Citizenship in Canada*. Montreal: Institute for Research in Public Policy.

Ryan, Claude. 2004. "In Place of a Foreword." In Douglas Farrow, ed., *Recognizing Religion in a Secular Society: Essays in Pluralism, Religion and Public Policy.* Montreal and Kingston: McGill-Queen's University Press.

Sharlet, Jeff. 2006. "Through a Glass, Darkly: How the Christian Right is Reimagining U.S. History." *Harper's Magazine,* December.

Shipman, Tim. 2006. "Diversity 'Threat to Communities.'" *Daily Mail,* October 10, p. 22.

Soroka, Stuart N., Richard Johnston and Keith Banting. 2007. "Ties That Bind? Social Cohesion and Diversity in Canada." In Keith Banting, Thomas J. Courchene and F. Leslie Seidle, eds., *Belonging? Diversity, Recognition and Shared Citizenship in Canada.* Montreal: Institute for Research in Public Policy.

Taylor, Charles. 1990. *Sources of the Self: The Making of the Modern Identity.* Cambridge: Harvard University Press.

Todd, Douglas. 2002. "Ruling on Gays 'Assault on Religion': Trinity Western University Hosts a Conference on Religious Freedom." *Vancouver Sun,* June 7, p. B3.

Valpy, Michael. 2004. "U.S. on Dangerous Course, Expert Warns." *Globe and Mail,* August 6, p. A6.

Disentangling the Debate

Will Kymlicka

At the heart of Janice Gross Stein's chapter in this book is a concern about potential conflicts between religious freedom and equality rights, particularly the equality rights of women and homosexuals. She worries that Canada has not achieved a proper balance between these values and, moreover, that we are too afraid to discuss the issue properly. While this is her basic concern, she connects it to a larger set of "worrying trends" in relation to immigrant integration. For example, she mentions the fear that newer immigrants are not doing as well economically as previous immigrants, that immigrant groups are becoming more segregated, and that the Canadian-born children of immigrants feel disaffected from Canada.

These are challenging and provocative ideas, which the various commentators herein have both elaborated and disputed in diverse ways. There are many areas of agreement and disagreement among the authors that are worth exploring, but the first question I want to ask is how Stein's two sets of concerns are related. What exactly is the connection between concerns about potential conflicts between religious freedom and equality rights, on one hand, and concerns about immigrant integration, on the other?

According to Stein, they are connected through the ideology and policy of multiculturalism. Rethinking and "deepening" multiculturalism is, she suggests, crucial both to resolving the religious freedom debate and to improving immigrant integration. I am not persuaded that the two debates are as closely connected as Stein supposes, or that she has correctly identified the role that multiculturalism plays in either debate.

DEFINING MULTICULTURALISM

In order to clarify what is at stake in these debates, it may help to distinguish three different senses of multiculturalism, which I will label multiculturalism as fact, as policy and as ethos.

The presence of ethnocultural diversity is clearly a fact about Canada—indeed, Leslie Laczko (1994) shows that we are a "statistical outlier" among the western democracies in the breadth of our ethnic, linguistic and religious diversity. In that sense we are a "multicultural" society, and becoming more so by the day as a result of our proactive immigration policy.

But countries can respond to the fact of diversity in many different ways. In some countries, the government seeks to suppress diversity through assimilationist policies that impose a common culture on all ethnocultural minorities. In other countries, public policies seek to privatize diversity, by excluding the expression of minority cultures and identities from the public sphere, while allowing for their expression in private life.

In Canada, however, we have adopted a policy of recognizing and accommodating ethnocultural diversity within our public institutions, and celebrating it as an important dimension of our collective life and collective identity. In this sense, we have multiculturalism as a policy, as well as a fact. This policy was first adopted in 1971, enshrined in law in the Canadian Multiculturalism Act of 1988, and given constitutional recognition in section 27 of the Constitution.

A number of specific programs are supported under this policy, including anti-racism campaigns (which are the largest single program); pilot programs on how to improve ethnic representation and cultural sensitivity in the schools, healthcare system, police, and museums; academic studies of the history of ethnic groups in Canada and their contemporary circumstances; funding for multi-ethnic festivals; and so on. (For a detailed examination of the actual programs that get funded, see McAndrew, Helly and Tessier 2005.) Critics have often trivialized and caricatured the multiculturalism policy as being exclusively about funding folkdances, but it has a strong political and economic dimension to it, targeting the treatment and representation of ethnic groups within public institutions. In this way, it is one component in a larger policy framework of human rights, anti-discrimination laws and employment equity programs.

The multiculturalism policy has been controversial since its inception in 1971, but retains very broad levels of public support (Dasko 2005), and has in fact multiplied and diffused. The initial multiculturalism policy was adopted by the federal government, but versions of it have subsequently been adopted by several provincial and municipal governments.[1]

The multiplication and diffusion of multiculturalism policies—what we can call multiculturalism's "long march through the institutions"—have in turn helped to promote a certain kind of multicultural ethos that shapes how Canadians think about and discuss issues of diversity. This ethos has spread far beyond the remit of official multiculturalism policies. Multiculturalism policies apply primarily to public institutions, and most private institutions and civil society organizations in Canada are under no legal duty to become more ethnically representative or culturally sensitive. And yet in many ways it is precisely in civil society that we can see the ethos of multiculturalism at work—in women's groups, church groups, environmental organizations, trade unions and professional associations, businesses, universities, neighbourhood associations, arts organizations and so on.

At its best, this multicultural ethos is one of inclusion: organizations reaching out to members of ethnic groups, inviting them to participate, taking their interests and perspectives into account, and reconsidering any norms or practices that are perceived by minorities as unfair or exclusionary. At its worst, this ethos can degenerate into either tokenism or a stifling sort of political correctness. Some organizations care more about the appearance of having minority representation than actually listening to new perspectives; others are so desperate to avoid giving offence to minorities that they avoid difficult topics entirely and close their eyes to real problems within minority communities, or in the relations between minorities and the larger society.

So multiculturalism in Canada is a fact, a policy and an ethos. Having made these preliminary distinctions, we can now return to Stein's two concerns and ask in what ways multiculturalism is implicated in them, either as the cause or as potential remedy.

FREEDOM OF RELIGION

Stein's first concern is with the potential conflict between freedom of religion and equality rights. Should religious organizations be allowed to discriminate against women or homosexuals in hiring or in providing services? Should church-run hospitals be forced to provide information on contraception and abortion? Should religious schools be exempted from sex education or civics education? Both religious freedom and equality are foundational values in the Canadian Charter of Rights and Freedoms, as they are in every western liberal democratic constitution, but how should we resolve conflicts between them?

This is indeed a serious issue, but it is not clear how it is related to either immigration or multiculturalism. As Stein herself notes, multiculturalism is a relatively recent idea, dating back to 1971, whereas debates about the scope of religious freedom go back centuries in the western liberal tradition and are found in every western country, whether or not they have a multiculturalism policy. Most western democracies have a long tradition of exempting religious organizations from laws that conflict with their core religious doctrines, although these exemptions are often subject to ongoing debates. These exemptions often predate the adoption of any multiculturalism policy, whether in Canada or elsewhere, and often have nothing to do with immigrants. Indeed, Stein's own examples of the conflict between religious freedom and equality rights typically involve white Christian groups—such as the evangelical Christian school in Quebec that seeks exemption from sex education, the evangelical Christian teachers' college in British Columbia that instructed future teachers to view homosexuality as a sin, others have mentioned the Catholic school board in Ontario that refused a gay student the right to attend his graduation prom, and so on. Similarly, virtually all of the (vast) jurisprudence in the United States on these issues involves attempts by white Christian religious groups to avoid the application of equality provisions for women, gays and other minorities.

So immigration and multiculturalism are clearly not the source of these conflicts: these conflicts would arise even if Canada had no recent immigrants or no multiculturalism policy. But perhaps the presence in Canada of a multiculturalism policy has affected the way these cases are decided in the courts, or how the public thinks about them. As I interpret her chapter, Stein believes that multiculturalism has somehow tipped the scales in favour of greater deference to religious freedom and against equality rights.

I disagree. Indeed, I think her own analysis of the problem shows that multiculturalism is a red herring in this debate. According to Stein, the age-old debate about the scope of religious freedom has changed in recent years as a result of two factors: (a) the rise of a "culture of rights" in the western liberal democracies founded on ideals of equality and non-discrimination, and (b) the rise of religious orthodoxy in all of the world's faiths (partly as a reaction against the liberal culture of rights). The former makes the state and society generally more likely to insist on equality norms, the latter makes religious groups more likely to demand greater exemptions from such norms. As a result, the scope for conflict has increased.

I think this analysis is basically correct as far as it goes, although I would put more weight on the growth of a culture of rights than on the growth in religious orthodoxy. Even if the beliefs and practices of religious groups have not changed, the rise of a culture of rights in the larger society, and the resulting efforts to promote gender equality and gay rights, would lead to conflicts. This indeed is how many religious believers describe the situation: they were happy with the status quo of earlier years, and it was only the aggressive promotion of a culture of rights by the larger society, not any newfound orthodoxy on their part, that upset the old status quo. And this seems to be the moral of Stein's own personal case study with her synagogue. As she tells the story, her synagogue has not become more orthodox in recent years—if anything, it has become more inclusive of women's participation. However, the changes have not been fast enough to keep up with the emerging norms of our new culture of rights. Various religious groups may appear to be becoming more conservative or orthodox, but in fact they are simply not keeping pace with a rapidly liberalizing public culture of rights.

In any event, the basic outlines of the problem are clear. What is less clear is how multiculturalism fits into the picture. In order to see this, we need to explore in more depth this idea of a culture of rights. Ideas of rights have a long history in western political thought, but what Stein refers to as the culture of rights is a distinctly modern phenomenon, tied to the postwar human rights revolution. Before World War II, western democracies explicitly endorsed a wide range of hierarchies among citizens, according second-class status to women, ethnic and racial minorities, homosexuals and others. These distinctions were formally embedded in legislation and enforced by public institutions. After the war, when the world recoiled from Hitler's murderous ideology of racial hierarchy, the human rights revolution adopted a new ideology of equal rights and non-discrimination.

The first effect of this human rights revolution was to delegitimize explicit discrimination by the state itself—for instance, racial segregation in public schools, or rules prohibiting women from serving on juries. But it quickly became clear that if citizens are to have true equality, the principle of equality needed to be both deepened within state institutions and broadened to apply to certain non-state institutions.

Within state institutions, equality for historically disadvantaged groups requires not only the removal of formal discrimination, but also reforms to make these institutions more accessible and welcoming—for example, through curriculum reform in public schools to remove gender and race biases; sensitivity training for police, healthcare workers and social service providers; the reassessment of hiring and promotion criteria that indirectly discriminate against women or minorities; employment equity programs to overcome the "chilly climate" that often affects women and minorities seeking public sector employment or advancement; and so on.

Equality rights must also be broadened to apply to the institutions of civil society. Even if people are treated equitably by state institutions, they cannot hope to achieve full equality if they remain discriminated against by private sector employers. And so legal requirements of non-discrimination have gradually been extended to private sector employers and landlords and to stores that serve the public. Indeed, the logic of the human rights revolution pushes us to extend equality rights ever deeper and broader into civil society. Consider private clubs: should the Rotary Club or Jaycees be required to admit women? Should the Boy Scouts be required to admit atheists? And what about churches? Should the Catholic church be required to allow women to become priests? Should the Mormon church be required to hire a homosexual as a janitor, if he is the best qualified?

There are powerful arguments for continually broadening and deepening the enforcement of equality rights. After all, even when the historical ideologies and practices of racial and gender inequality are (more or less) removed from public institutions, they remain durably entrenched in many aspects of society, and we cannot remain indifferent to the way these continue to affect the life chances of citizens.

And yet we have to stop somewhere. Pushing equality norms all the way down would effectively abolish any meaningful right of religious freedom, or indeed of freedom of association more generally. As a result, the courts in the US and Canada have developed a battery of tests for resolving this question. For example, it matters whether the organization in question is small or large (intimate associations are more likely to be exempt); whether the organization plays a major role in the economic life of the community (in the US, it was successfully argued that women could not achieve equality without being admitted to the Jaycees, given the central role that the latter play in establishing business contacts); whether the organization receives public funding or delivers public services; or whether the practice of discrimination is essential to the stated purpose of the organization.

There is a fascinating and continually evolving jurisprudence on these issues, and in general there is a clear trend toward extending equality norms deeper into civil society.[2] But not always. In particular, the courts have been reluctant to intervene in two specific areas:

religious organizations and the family. In these two contexts, unlike other private sector institutions and civil society organizations, the courts have generally avoided any attempt to impose equality norms. Of course, the criminal code sets limitations in these two spheres, prohibiting child abuse or violence. But, as Stein puts it, in these two contexts "we draw a line at violence and abuse, manage these violations of rights through the criminal code" but "let almost everything else" go unnoticed.

Stein is worried that giving a carte blanche to religious organizations reflects a failure to take our equality norms seriously, and that the effects of this failure may get worse if religious orthodoxy grows. More and more inequalities may get smuggled in and protected under the rubric of religious freedom.

This then is the backdrop for Stein's concern about the culture of rights and its potential conflict with religious freedom. It is not entirely clear what her proposed solution is, and I will return to that later. But we still need to sort out the role of multiculturalism in the debate. If there is a growing conflict between religious orthodoxy and the culture of rights, is multiculturalism an ally of the former or the latter?

Stein implies that multiculturalism buttresses claims made by religious orthodoxy, and thereby impedes the progress of a culture of rights. Indeed, the passage I quoted earlier actually states: "we draw a line at violence and abuse ... but *let almost everything else fall under the rubric of multiculturalism*" [my italics]. According to Stein, then, it is multiculturalism that explains why we have privileged religious freedom over equality rights. Multiculturalism provides a pretext or justification for religious organizations to avoid the broadening and deepening of equality rights.

I disagree. There is indeed a potential conflict between the traditional deference to religious freedom and the newer movement to broaden and deepen equality rights. But multiculturalism as a legal principle and as public policy in Canada falls clearly into the latter camp. Multiculturalism in Canada was part and parcel of the larger process of liberalization in the 1960s and '70s in Canada, along with feminist, disability and gay rights movements, all of which were committed to redressing inherited forms of inequality and stigmatization. Like all of these civil rights movements, multiculturalism was premised on the assumption that inherited ethnic and racial hierarchies could not be effectively redressed solely on the basis of formal non-discrimination within state institutions. Instead, true equality for ethnic groups required both deepening equality within public institutions (for example, by adopting multicultural curricula in public schools or multicultural programming in public media) and broadening equality within the larger society (such as by promoting anti-racism campaigns or working with private sector and civil society organizations to become more inclusive). Indeed, the multiculturalism policy has been one of the prime vehicles in the federal government for thinking about the broadening and deepening of ethnic and racial equality.

Anyone who appeals to the multiculturalism policy, therefore, is appealing to a political discourse and legal framework that promotes a culture of rights. Consider the preamble to the Canadian Multiculturalism Act. It begins by saying that because the government of Canada is committed to civil liberties, particularly the freedom of individuals "to make the life that the individual is able and wishes to have," and because it is committed to equality, particularly racial equality and gender equality, and because of its international human rights obligations, particularly the international convention against racial discrimination, therefore it is adopting a policy of multiculturalism. It goes on, in the main text, to reiterate human rights norms as part of the substance of the multiculturalism policy. You could hardly ask for a clearer statement that multiculturalism is to be understood as an integral part of the human rights revolution, and as an extension of, not a brake on, the culture of rights. There is not a whiff of support for cultural conservatism or religious orthodoxy in this statement.

These formulations are obviously intended as an instruction to the relevant political actors, from minority activists to bureaucrats, that multiculturalism must be understood as a policy inspired by norms of liberal equality, and as one part of a broader struggle for equality, including gender equality. Nor was this left to chance, or to the good will of political actors. The Multiculturalism Act is located squarely within the larger framework of liberal democratic constitutionalism, and hence is legally subject to the same constitutional standards of equality rights as any other federal policy. Any federal action done in the name of multiculturalism must respect the requirements of the Charter, as interpreted and enforced by judicial bodies such as the Canadian Human Rights Commission and the Supreme Court of Canada.

So the way in which multiculturalism in Canada has been legally defined makes clear that it does not exist outside the framework of equality rights and human rights jurisprudence, or as an exception to it, or a deviation from it. Rather, it is firmly embedded within that framework. It is defined as flowing from human rights norms, as embodying those norms, and as enforceable through judicial institutions whose mandate is to uphold those norms.

In that sense, the multiculturalism policy is part and parcel of the very culture of rights that religious orthodoxy opposes.[3] And indeed most conservative religious groups oppose the adoption of multiculturalism. Stein talks about the way orthodox religious groups have opposed gender equality and gay rights, but she does not mention the fact that such groups have also opposed multiculturalism, and for the same reason—namely, that it requires groups to extend equal respect (or at least tolerance) to people whose way of life conflicts with their traditional teachings. Orthodox groups resist having to teach their children multiculturalism for the same reason they resist having to teach gender equality and gay rights—they don't want their children exposed to materials that portray alternative ways of life in a sympathetic light, and thereby potentially undermine their adherence to orthodoxy.[4]

So I don't think it is correct to say that we ignore or condone inequality within religious organizations because it falls under the rubric of multiculturalism. There is nothing in the multiculturalism policy that supports claims for religious exemptions from equality rights, and Stein does not cite any examples of the multiculturalism policy supporting such claims. Given its mandate, the multiculturalism policy is eligible to fund women's groups seeking to challenge religious orthodoxy in the name of equality rights, and has indeed done so, but it has no mandate to fund orthodox organizations seeking to limit equality rights, and has not done so.

Orthodox groups are quite aware of the fact that the multiculturalism policy offers them little support. When they seek to blunt the application of equality rights, they rarely appeal to the policy of multiculturalism.[5] Rather, they invoke more longstanding ideas of religious freedom—of *libertas ecclesiae*—that go back at least to the conflicts between popes and emperors in the eleventh century, and that are recognized in most western constitutional orders as the basis for according special protection to religious associations beyond those extended to other private associations. On the basis of these longstanding ideas of religious freedom, orthodox groups oppose the deepening or broadening of newfangled ideas of equality, whether of gender, sexuality or multiculturalism.

In short, I agree with Stein's concern that we need to be aware of potential conflicts between religious freedom and a culture of rights. But the real issue, in my view, is the pre-modern legal doctrine of *libertas ecclesaie*, which gives religious organizations broad exemptions from equality rights, not the post-modern Multiculturalism Act, which firmly endorses the norms and principles of equality. To say that we ignore violations of equality within religious organizations "under the rubric of multiculturalism" is, I think, wrong as a matter of legal history and as a matter of contemporary public policy.

But perhaps this misses the real point of Stein's critique. At times, it seems that her concern is not with the multiculturalism policy per se—as I said, she gives no examples of the multiculturalism policy supporting religious exemptions from equality rights—but rather with what I am calling the ethos of multiculturalism. In particular, Stein is worried that we have developed a political culture in which we avoid asking hard questions about the violation of equality rights within ethnic and religious groups for fear of giving offence. The official policy may strongly endorse equality rights, but this is not much help if people are reluctant to raise questions publicly about whether those rights are in fact being respected.

This raises interesting questions about the relationship between multiculturalism as policy and multiculturalism as ethos. It may well be true that in some cases the ethos of multiculturalism in Canada has served to suppress debates about how best to achieve the original emancipatory aims of the policy. Of course, as Haroon Siddiqui notes, there have been lots of public debates in Canada recently about potential conflicts between religion and equality rights. But too often these debates have been initiated by right-wing commentators as thinly disguised strategies for attacking immigrants, particularly Muslims, often accompanied by apocalyptic predictions about how Canada's experiment in multiculturalism is on the verge of collapsing. Such commentators raise these issues in order to discredit multiculturalism.

Stein is careful to emphasize that this is not her agenda. She insists that the phenomenon of religious orthodoxy applies to all groups, not just to Muslims or other recent immigrants, and that the solution involves strengthening multiculturalism, not abandoning it. She wants a more vibrant and informed public debate on these issues precisely in order to "deepen" our experiment in liberal multiculturalism. I share that hope. But just for that reason, it is important not to misdiagnose the problem. The Canadian Multiculturalism Act, and the multiculturalism programs funded under it, is an ally of the culture of rights she endorses, not an enemy. It provides a set of legal principles, institutional access points and policy levers that have allowed ethnic and racial groups in Canada to broaden and deepen their pursuit of equality. It has not served as a rubric under which groups can seek exemptions from equality. In short, it is a resource to be drawn upon, not an obstacle to be overcome.

IMMIGRANT INTEGRATION

This brings me to Stein's second concern, about the "worrying trends" in immigrant integration. Here again, I share her concern, but disagree with the way she connects it to issues of multiculturalism.

That there are worrying trends regarding immigrant integration is impossible now to dispute. For example, there is evidence that recent immigrants are not faring as well economically as earlier cohorts of immigrants. But multiculturalism is not the main factor at play here. A more important factor is the mismatch between the points system under which immigrants are selected and their subsequent access to the labour market. We admit immigrants on the basis of their foreign credentials and work experience, but these credentials and experiences are not properly recognized in Canada. This is partly the result of provincial licensing and accreditation policies, which refuse to recognize foreign credentials, and partly the result of the hiring policies of private sector employers, which unduly discount foreign work experience. These are serious problems that we desperately need to address, but they fall outside the jurisdiction of the federal multiculturalism policy.

These problems primarily affect the first generation, and hence are transitional. Insofar as the children of immigrants acquire their education and work experience in Canada, one can expect that they will do better than their parents in educational attainment and in the labour market. And indeed that appears to be true. There is disturbing evidence, however, discussed in Michael Valpy's chapter, that this second generation faces other obstacles. It appears that, even if they do well in terms of education and income, second-generation visible minority Canadians often have lower feelings of belonging to Canada than other Canadians, largely due to the perception that they are discriminated against (Reitz and Banerjee 2007).

This clearly does fall under the remit of the multiculturalism policy. Indeed, the policy has funded many programs over the years intended precisely to combat discrimination and to promote a feeling of belonging among visible minorities. Not surprisingly, therefore, the results of these studies have widely been interpreted as a failure of the multiculturalism policy, and commentators have wondered if we are sleepwalking into the sort of ethnic segregation and racialized poverty that characterizes immigrant groups in so many European countries.

However, it is important to set these findings in context. Recent polling data contain some pleasant surprises as well as some disappointments, and we need to fine-tune our evaluation of what is working and what is not. For example, while visible minorities express lower feelings of "belonging" to Canada than white Canadians, they do not express lower feelings of "pride" in Canada. (Actually, they express higher levels of pride.) And, if one controls for years of residence in Canada, visible minorities are just as likely to participate in "bridging" networks that include people from different ethnic and religious backgrounds and to participate in the political system (Howe 2007; Soroka, Johnston and Banting 2007).

Perhaps most important for Stein's argument, there are no statistically significant differences across ethnic groups in Canada regarding support for "Charter values," such as gay rights or women working outside the home. There may be a rise in religious orthodoxy around the world, but there is no evidence that it is leading to a cleavage along ethnic or racial lines within Canada. There are divisions between liberals and conservatives within each ethnic and racial group, but there is no "clash of civilizations" between different groups in Canada.

So while we should not ignore the disaffection that arises among groups that perceive themselves to be victims of discrimination, we also shouldn't extrapolate this into a more general failure of immigrant integration. On the contrary, taking all the data together, one can plausibly conclude that "the country seems to be successfully facing the challenges" of immigration (Soroka, Johnston and Banting 2007, 642). Whatever the imperfections of our approach, Canada continually scores better than other countries on basic measures of immigrant participation, belonging, trust, and so on.

While some of this is undoubtedly due to the fact that we cherry-pick our immigrants, selecting the most skilled, there is good reason to believe that our multiculturalism policy also plays a role in our comparative success. Consider the fascinating study done by Irene Bloemraad (2006) comparing Vietnamese immigrants in Boston and Toronto. There were virtually no relevant differences in the demographic characteristics of the Vietnamese immigrants who ended up in Toronto rather than Boston—they arrived with comparable levels of education, work experience, language fluency, and so on. Yet the Vietnamese in Toronto have integrated much better and are more actively participating in Canadian public life. There are of course many possible explanations for this difference other than the presence of Canada's multiculturalism policies (such as labour markets, political party structures, etc.), but Bloemraad systematically canvases the alternative explanations and concludes that multiculturalism policies were indeed a crucial part of the story. These policies encouraged and enabled the Vietnamese community to participate more quickly and more effectively in mainstream Canadian institutions. According to Bloemraad, the same pattern applies to Portuguese immigrants to Toronto and

Boston as well—they arrived with similar demographic characteristics, but the Portuguese immigrants in Toronto have integrated better, due in part to Canadian multiculturalism.

In short, Stein's worries that our "shallow multiculturalism" is impeding the political integration of immigrants, or inhibiting their internalization of Charter values, seems unsupported by the evidence. There is a strong and durable consensus across ethnic and racial lines on basic Charter values and immigrants continue to be smoothly integrated into it, in part because our multiculturalism policy facilitates that integration. In confronting the ongoing challenges of economic disadvantage and discrimination, we should not misidentify the target and abandon a model of political integration that is in fact working well.

CONCLUSION

According to John Ibbitson, "it is wrong to say that political correctness, or a desire not to offend, is keeping us from facing a growing threat. There is no threat, pure and simple." I broadly agree, but would put the point slightly differently. There may be no threat, but the adoption of multiculturalism does involve a gamble. It rests on what Nancy Rosenblum (1998, 55–61) calls the "liberal expectancy"—that is, the hope and expectation that liberal democratic values will grow over time and take firm root across ethnic, racial and religious lines, within both majority and minority groups.

This liberal expectancy rests, in part, on the assumption that the public structures and principles of a liberal democracy exert a kind of gravitational pull on the beliefs and practices of ethnic and religious groups. As Rosenblum notes, this metaphor of gravitational pull—an all-pervasive but invisible force—obscures rather than reveals the actual mechanisms at work, and many discussions of the liberal expectancy have a somewhat mysterious air to them. However, we know that such a process has indeed operated historically. When Catholics and Jews first started arriving in the United States in the nineteenth century, for example, it was widely believed that their conservative and patriarchal beliefs and authoritarian practices precluded them from truly embracing liberal democracy. And yet most religious groups in America have become liberalized, gradually incorporating norms of individual freedom, tolerance and sexual equality into their own self-understanding. Similarly, there were doubts about whether earlier waves of immigrants to the US and Canada from southern or eastern Europe, where liberal democracy had never taken root, could truly internalize liberal democratic values. Yet today these groups are often seen as some of the most loyal defenders of constitutional principles.

These earlier experiences of the liberal expectancy in action helped generate confidence in Canada that a truly liberal democratic form of multiculturalism is possible, and that multiculturalism can facilitate the deepening and broadening of a culture of rights. This confidence is now under attack. Allan Gregg's 2006 article in *The Walrus* is among the best-known examples of a new anxiety about the liberal expectancy that is rippling through Canada. And, at times, Stein seems to share this anxiety.

In my view, however, this anxiety is unwarranted in Canada. We have every reason to believe that the basic processes underpinning the liberal expectancy are still at work here. We undoubtedly have racism, economic inequality and disaffection. But on Stein's underlying question of whether immigrants are integrating into our culture of rights, and whether multiculturalism is facilitating that integration, we can and should remain confident.

And this brings me back full circle to Stein's opening question about the balance between religious freedom and equality rights. As she notes, these are hard cases, and there is no simple formula for deciding when to intervene in religious associations in order to deepen and broaden the culture of rights. But one important factor, I believe, is whether we have confidence that the liberal expectancy is holding. In much of Europe, this confidence is completely lacking, particularly in relation to Muslim immigrants, and so public authorities feel they need to intervene publicly and continuously within Muslim communities to test their adherence to liberal values, and to monitor and police any deviations from these values. State officials feel they need to intervene now, because they fear that things will only get worse as time goes on. And so they insist that Muslims publicly proclaim that they are, say, "British first," and publicly renounce any aspect of Islam that state officials view as illiberal.

But if we believe that the liberal expectancy is holding, and that immigrants converge on Charter values the longer they reside in Canada (as all the evidence shows), then we can afford to take a more subtle approach. We must protect vulnerable citizens from abuse and violence, whatever their race or religion, and we must enforce the rule of law. And we should insist that organizations receiving public funds comply with non-discrimination standards. But we do not need to continuously test or provoke minorities, as is the fashion these days in Europe, whether in the form of the Mohammed cartoons in Denmark or the veil law in France. (Or, sadly, in the anti-stoning bylaw in Hérouxville, Quebec.[6]) This sort of provocation is self-defeating. If we tell immigrants that we don't trust them, and that we are monitoring their every word and reaction for hints of disloyalty or illiberalism, they will not feel that their political participation is welcomed and their political integration will be delayed, if not derailed entirely. By contrast, if we trust that immigrants will, over time, converge on Charter values, and if we welcome their political participation on that basis, it is more likely that they will in fact integrate. In that sense, the liberal expectancy can be self-fulfilling—successful political integration into a culture of rights is more likely to occur if people believe it will occur.

And we can consider reasonable accommodations in a pragmatic way. For example, if some religiously conservative parents want their children to have access to sex-segregated phys-ed classes or swimming times, it may be prudent to accept this, since it is better to keep their children in the public schools than have them withdraw into home schooling. We can safely rely on the gravitational pull of liberal democratic institutions to diffuse a culture of rights over time, but only if people are in fact participating in those institutions.

Here again, there is no magic formula for determining when such accommodations are prudent, and when they constitute impermissible violations of the spirit or letter of equality. There is lots of room for reasonable debate. But, like Ibbitson's, my sense is that when the debate is done, we probably would not (and should not) dramatically change the way we draw the bounds of religious freedom. Our long-term goal should indeed be to deepen and broaden the culture of rights. But the gravitational pull of liberal democratic institutions may be a more effective tool in this regard than aggressive intervention into every nook and cranny of civil society.

NOTES

1 Actually, the very first multiculturalism policy in Canada was adopted in Alberta, just before the federal government's 1971 policy statement.

2 For an interesting discussion of the evolving jurisprudence in American cases, see Spinner-Halev 2000, ch. 7.

3 For a more detailed discussion of how multiculturalism, both in its origins and legal formulation, is tied to broader processes of liberalization and human rights, see Kymlicka 2007a, ch. 4.

4 As Michael Adams (1997, 2000) has shown, social and religious conservatives in Canada link multiculturalism, feminism and gay rights as objectionable manifestations of permissive liberalism and secular humanism. Conversely, as Rhoda Howard-Hassman (2002) has shown, liberals and social democrats in Canada link multiculturalism, feminism and gay rights as desirable manifestations of the human rights revolution. For both camps, multiculturalism is seen as part and parcel of the culture of rights, although they disagree about whether that is good or bad. Of course, once multiculturalism is in place, conservative religious groups that initially opposed it may attempt to find ways to take advantage of it—see Davies 1999 for an interesting example.

5 The recent debate about sharia-based family law tribunals in Ontario may seem like a counter-example. Several media reports portrayed this as an example of Muslim organizations invoking the multiculturalism policy to gain an exemption from gender equality rights under Canadian law. However, this is a complete misrepresentation of the actual case. The proposal to establish sharia-based family law arbitration did not involve seeking an exemption from existing family law, let alone an exemption based on multiculturalism. It simply took advantage of the provisions of the (poorly drafted) 1991 Arbitration Act, which allowed anyone to establish private arbitration with minimal restrictions or oversight. Had this act not existed, one could imagine a Muslim organization requesting a special exemption from family law in order to apply gender-biased sharia norms and defending this request in the name of multiculturalism. However, any such request would have had no chance of succeeding. To repeat, there is nothing in the multiculturalism policy (or the Multiculturalism Act) that would sup-

port such a request, and I know of no examples where the multiculturalism program has endorsed or funded any such proposal that would jeop-
ardize equality rights. This was a problem with the Arbitration Act, not the
Multiculturalism Act. For further discussion, see Kymlicka 2007b.

6 In January 2007, a small town in rural Quebec adopted a bylaw instructing
would-be immigrants that it is forbidden, *inter alia*, to stone women or
burn them with acid, or for women to wear a veil (see Moore 2007).

REFERENCES

Adams, Michael. 1997. *Sex in the Snow: Canadian Social Values at the End
of the Millennium*. Toronto: Penguin.

Adams, Michael. 2000. *Better Happy Than Rich? Canadians, Money and
the Meaning of Life*. Toronto: Penguin.

Bloemraad, Irene. 2006. *Becoming a Citizen: Incorporating Immigrants and
Refugees in the United States and Canada*. Berkeley: University of
California Press.

Dasko, Donna. 2005. "Public Attitudes Towards Multiculturalism and Bilingualism in Canada." In Margaret Adsett, Caroline Mallandain and
Shannon Stettner, eds., *Canadian and French Perspectives on Diversity: Conference Proceedings*. October 16, 2003. Ottawa: Department
of Canadian Heritage. dsp-psd.pwgsc.gc.ca/Collection/CH36-4-1-
2004E.pdf (March 2007).

Davies, Scott. 1999. "From Moral Duty to Cultural Rights: A Case Study of
Political Framing in Education." *Sociology of Education*, vol. 72,
no. 1, pp. 1–21.

Gregg, Allan. 2006. "Identity Crisis. Multiculturalism: A Twentieth-Cen-
tury Dream Becomes A Twenty-First-Century Conundrum." *Walrus
Magazine*, March, vol. 3, no. 2, p. 38.

Howard-Hassmann, Rhoda. 2003. *Compassionate Canadians: Civic Leaders Discuss Human Rights*. Toronto: University of Toronto Press.

Howe, Paul. 2007. "The Political Engagement of New Canadians: A Com-
parative Perspective." In Keith Banting, Thomas J. Courchene and
F. Leslie Seidle, eds., *Belonging? Diversity, Recognition and Shared
Citizenship in Canada*. Montreal: Institute for Research on Public
Policy.

Kymlicka, Will. 2007a. *Multicultural Odysseys: Navigating the New International Politics of Diversity*. Oxford: Oxford University Press.

Kymlicka, Will. 2007b. "Testing the Bounds of Liberal Multiculturalism?
The Sharia Debate in Ontario." *Raison Publique*, forthcoming.

Laczko, Leslie S. 1994. "Canada's Pluralism in Comparative Perspective." *Ethnic and Racial Studies*, vol. 17, no. 1, pp. 20–41.

McAndrew, Marie, Denise Helly and Caroline Tessier. 2005. "Pour un débat éclairé sur la politique canadienne du multiculturalisme: une analyse de la nature des organismes et des projets subventionnés (1983–2002)." *Politique et Sociétes*, vol. 24, no. 1, pp. 49–71.

Moore, Dene. 2007. "Quebec Town Bans Kirpans, Stoning Women." *Globe and Mail,* January 30, p. A12.

Reitz, Jeffrey and Rupa Banerjee. 2007. "Racial Inequality, Social Cohesion and Policy Issues in Canada." In Keith Banting, Thomas J. Courchene and F. Leslie Seidle, eds., *Belonging? Diversity, Recognition and Shared Citizenship in Canada*. Montreal: Institute for Research on Public Policy.

Rosenblum, Nancy. 1998. *Membership and Morals: The Personal Uses of Pluralism in America*. Princeton: Princeton University Press.

Soroka, Stuart, Richard Johnston and Keith Banting. 2007. "Ties That Bind? Social Cohesion and Diversity in Canada." In Keith Banting, Thomas J. Courchene and F. Leslie Seidle, eds., *Belonging? Diversity, Recognition and Shared Citizenship in Canada*. Montreal: Institute for Research in Public Policy.

Spinner-Halev, Jeff. 2000. *Surviving Diversity: Religion and Democratic Citizenship*. Baltimore: Johns Hopkins University Press.

Contributors

David Robertson Cameron, a Fellow of the Royal Society of Canada, is chair and professor of political science at the University of Toronto, where he served as vice-president from 1985 to 1987. He has divided his time between public service (federally and provincially) and academic life. For the government of Canada, he has served as Assistant Secretary to Cabinet for Strategic and Constitutional Planning and was assistant undersecretary of State from 1979 to 1985. For Ontario, he was Deputy Minister of Intergovernmental Affairs from 1987 to 1990. His recent publications include *Cycling into Saigon: The 1995 Conservative Transition in Ontario* (2000), with Graham White; *Disability and Federalism: Comparing Different Approaches to Full Participation* (2001), with Fraser Valentine; and *Street Protests and Fantasy Parks: Globalization, Culture and Society* (2002), with Janice Gross Stein.

The Honourable Frank Iacobucci is counsel with Torys LLP and chair of Torstar Corporation and a director of Tim Hortons Inc. He is also chair of the Higher Education Quality Council of Ontario. He has taught at and was dean of the Faculty of Law of the University of Toronto, and served as the university's vice-president of internal affairs as well as provost and, from September 2004 to June 2005, was interim president. In 1985 he was appointed deputy minister of Justice and deputy attorney general for Canada; in 1988, chief justice of the Federal Court of Canada; and from 1991 to 2004, a justice of the Supreme Court of

Canada. In 2005, he was the federal representative in the negotiations leading to a comprehensive agreement to resolve the legacy of Indian Residential Schools. He is also a member of the Ontario Law Commission and, in December 2006, was appointed commissioner to lead an inquiry into the conduct of Canadian officials regarding certain individuals. A recipient of numerous awards and honours in Canada and abroad, he has authored or edited numerous books, articles, and commentaries on a variety of subjects.

John Ibbitson has written on provincial, national and American politics since joining *The Globe and Mail* in 1999. He has also written numerous books on politics and public policy, the most recent being *The Polite Revolution: Perfecting the Canadian Dream* (2005). From 2002 to 2007 he wrote the political affairs column for the *Globe*, based in Ottawa, before moving to Washington to write commentary on American politics and society. He is also a well-known author of novels for young readers, including *1812: Jeremy's War* (1991) and *Water Music*, to be published in 2008 by Kidscan Press.

Will Kymlicka holds the Canada Research Chair in Political Philosophy at Queen's University and is a fellow of the Royal Society of Canada, the Canadian Institute of Advanced Research and the Trudeau Foundation. He is the author of six books published by Oxford University Press: *Liberalism, Community and Culture* (1989), *Contemporary Political Philosophy: An Introduction* (1990; second edition 2002), *Multicultural Citizenship: A Liberal Theory of Minority Right* (1995), *Finding Our Way: Rethinking Ethnocultural Relations in Canada* (1998), *Politics in the Vernacular: Nationalism, Multiculturalism and Citizenship* (2001) and *Multicultural Odysseys: Navigating the New International Politics of Diversity* (2007). His works have been translated into 30 languages.

John Meisel, of Czech origin, is the Sir Edward Peacock Professor of Political Science Emeritus at Queen's University. He is a Companion of the Order of Canada, a former president of the Royal Society of Canada and a one-time chair of the Canadian Radio and Telecommunication Commission of Canada. Except for visiting professorships at Yale University and in the United Kingdom, he spent his whole academic life at Queen's, where he pioneered studies of elections and political parties, the role of government in the arts, the politics of regulation and challenges to national cohesion. Teaching, research, writing and nature

have been his passions and he finds it hard not to get involved in issues affecting the common weal.

Haroon Siddiqui is a columnist for the *Toronto Star*. He is a former editorial page editor, national editor, news editor and correspondent. He
has covered, among other events, the Soviet invasion and occupation
of Afghanistan, the Iranian revolution, the Iran–Iraq war and, lately, the
emergence of China and India as global economic powers. He has written extensively on multiculturalism and Canada's changing demo-
graphy. Author of *Being Muslim* (2006), a study on the impact of September 11 on Muslims around the world, he is a recipient of both the
Order of Canada and the Order of Ontario.

Janice Gross Stein is the Belzberg Professor of Conflict Management in
the Department of Political Science and the director of the Munk Centre for International Studies at the University of Toronto. She is a Fellow of the Royal Society of Canada and a member of the Order of
Canada. She is the author of *The Cult of Efficiency* (2001) and the co-
author of *Networks of Knowledge: Innovation in International Learning* (2000) and *The Unexpected War: Canada in Kandahar* (2007). She
is co-editor of *Street Protests and Fantasy Parks: Globalization, Culture
and Society* (2001) and a contributor to *Canada by Picasso: The Faces of
Federalism* (2006). She was the Massey lecturer in 2001 and a Trudeau
Fellow. She was awarded the Molson Prize by the Canada Council for
an outstanding contribution by a social scientist to public debate. She
is an Honorary Foreign Member of the American Academy of Arts and
Sciences. In 2006, she was awarded an Honorary Doctorate of Laws
by the University of Alberta and the University of Cape Breton.

Michael Valpy is a senior writer for *The Globe and Mail*. He began his
journalistic career in Vancouver and became associate editor and national affairs columnist of *The Vancouver Sun*. For *The Globe and Mail*,
he has been a member of the editorial board, Ottawa national political
columnist, Africa correspondent, deputy managing editor and a national columnist on social policy and urban issues. He is co-author of
two books on the Constitution—*The National Deal* (1982) and *To Match
a Dream* (1998)—and co-author with *Globe* colleague Erin Anderssen
of *The New Canada: A Profile of the Next Generation* (2004). He has
produced public affairs documentaries for CBC Radio, written for
Maclean's, Elm Street, Canadian Living, Literary Review of Canada,

Time Canada and *Policy Options* magazines and won three National Newspaper Awards—two for foreign reporting and one for an examination of how the schools cope with children of dysfunctional families. In 1997, Canada's Trent University awarded him an honorary doctorate for his journalism.

Index